Standardized Test Preparation Book for Reading and Language Arts

Teacher's Edition

Grade 1

Orlando Boston Dallas Chicago San Diego

Visit *The Learning Site!*
www.harcourtschool.com

Printed in the United States of America

ISBN 0-15-320929-1

9 073 2007 2006 2005

Contents

INTRODUCTION

This book prepares students for the reading and language arts subtests of widely used achievement tests. At the Primary 1 level, these subtests are Word Reading, Word Study Skills, Reading Comprehension, Spelling, Language, and Listening.

The student book is organized in the following three sections to lead students from scaffolded practice to independent performance.

1. **Modeled Instruction** This section explains each kind of test item. It includes skill-building lessons, models for choosing the answers to test items, and practice items with specific test-taking tips.
2. **Guided Practice** This is a practice section with tips related to specific items.
3. **Practice Test** This section simulates the actual test.

This Teacher's Edition begins with the **Directions for Administering**. The directions follow the order of the sections in the student book.

The Teacher's Edition also includes a **Student Profile** for recording students' scores as they progress through the book (see page T23). Use the chart below to help you plan administration of the **Practice Test**.

PRACTICE TEST PACING CHART

	Primary 1	Primary 2	Primary 3
	End of grade 1; beginning of grade 2	End of grade 2; beginning of gradc 3	End of grade 3; beginning of grade 4
Word Reading	24 items 30 mins		
Word Study Skills	25 items 15 mins	24 items 15 mins	
Reading Vocabulary		24 items 16 mins	32 items 20 mins
Reading Comprehension	29 items 30 mins	24 items 25 mins	45 items 40 mins
Spelling	30 items 25 mins	17 items 15 mins	10 items 10 mins
Language	28 items 25 mins	33 items 30 mins	41 items 40 mins
Listening	30 items 25 mins	29 items 20 mins	17 items 12 mins

Directions for Administering

Use with pages 9–11.

Read through the Modeled Instruction with students. Then have them do the sample item.

SAY **In the shaded box you see a picture of a woman on a street. Below the picture you see the words *store . . . telephone . . . party*. Which word tells about the picture?**

Continue in the same way for each picture. Help students complete items 1 through 15.

Use with pages 12–13.

Read through the Modeled Instruction with students. Then read to them the sample item.

SAY **In the shaded box you see the words *running . . . birthday . . . landed.* Which of these words has two words in it?**

Continue in the same way for items 1 through 8.

Use with pages 14–15.

Read through the Modeled Instruction with students. Then read to them the sample item.

SAY **You see three words. Each word has a different ending. I will say one of the words and use it in a sentence. Then you will find the word. Mark next to *singer*. The *singer* has a good voice. *Singer*.**

Have students work items 1 through 8 as you read each sentence.

1 **Mark next to *added*. We *added* pennies to find the total. *Added*.**

2 **Mark next to *thicker*. The *thicker* book took longer to read. *Thicker*.**

3 **Mark next to *thanked*. I *thanked* my guests for coming. *Thanked*.**

4 **Mark next to *digging*. The dog was *digging* a hole under the fence. *Digging*.**

5 **Mark next to *nicest*. The *nicest* gift is that you came. *Nicest*.**

6 **Mark next to *walked*. We *walked* until our feet hurt. *Walked*.**

7 **Mark next to *louder*. The *louder* music hurts my ears. *Louder*.**

8 **Mark next to *shortly*. My brother will be here *shortly*. *Shortly*.**

Use with page 16.

Read through the Modeled Instruction with students. Then read to them the sample item.

SAY **In the sample, you see the words *you're . . . you'd . . . you'll.* Mark the space under the word that means *you would. You would* go to the show if you could. *You would.***

Have students work items 1 through 4 as you read each sentence.

1 **Which one means the same as *she would*? *She would* want to help you. *She would.***

2 **Which one means the same as *we are*? *We are* happy to join you. *We are.***

3 **Which one means the same as *who is*? *Who is* your favorite singer? *Who is*?**

4 **Which one means the same as *it is*? *It is* fun to go to the movies. *It is.***

Use with pages 17–19.

Read through the Modeled Instruction with students. Then read to them the sample item.

SAY **You see four words. The first word is *tool.* The letter *t* in *tool* has a line under it. Which word has the same /t/ sound as the letter *t* in *tool*?**

Have students work items 1 through 15 as you read each word.

Use with page 20.

Read through the Modeled Instruction with students. Then read to them the sample item. Have students work items 1 and 2 on their own.

Use with pages 21–22.

Read through the Modeled Instruction with students. Then read to them the sample item. Have students work items 1 through 4 on their own.

Use with pages 23–26.

Read through the Modeled Instruction with students. Then read to them the sample item. Have students work items 1 through 6 on their own.

Use with pages 27–28.

Read through the Modeled Instruction with students. Then read to them the sample item.

SAY **_Said_. I could not hear what John _said_. _Said_. Find the correct spelling of _said_. Mark your answer.**

Have students work items 1 through 12 as you read each sentence.

1 **_Does_. She _does_ not live here. _Does_.**

2 **_When_. We will leave _when_ Pat arrives. _When_.**

3 **_Look_. Let's help Jan _look_ for her gloves. _Look_.**

4 **_Are_. Where _are_ the balls? _Are_.**

5 **_Happy_. Are you _happy_ about the party? _Happy_.**

6 **_Pitch_. Will you _pitch_ the ball to me? _Pitch_.**

7 **_Know_. You _know_ the right answer. _Know_.**

8 **_Light_. The sun gives us _light_. _Light_.**

9 **_Dish_. Mom handed me the _dish_. _Dish_.**

10 **_City_. We live in the _city_, not the country. _City_.**

11 **_One_. I have only _one_ cookie. _One_.**

12 **_Time_. What _time_ is recess? _Time_.**

Use with pages 29–30.

Read through the Modeled Instruction with students. Then read to them the sample item.

SAY **"Where is my book." How should the underlined part be written? Mark the space for your answer.**

Read items 1 through 5 with students, emphasizing the underlined words. Have them mark the space that shows how the underlined part of the sentence should be written.

Use with pages 31–32.

Read through the Modeled Instruction with students. Then read to them the sample item.

SAY **"The dog barked. At the cat." How should these groups of words be written to make a complete and correct sentence? Should they be written _The dog barked at the cat. . . . The dog barking at the cat. . . ._ or is this a complete and correct sentence _The way it is_? Mark your answer.**

Continue in the same way. Read items 1 through 4 with students as you did the sample.

Use with pages 33–34.

Read through the Modeled Instruction with students. Then read to them the sample item. Read items 1 and 2 as you did the sample.

Use with page 35.

Read through the Modeled Instruction with students. Then read to them the sample item.

SAY **Look at the words in the box: *dog . . . man . . . table*. Which word comes first in A-B-C order? Is it *dog, man,* or *table*?**

Read items 1 and 2 with students as you did the sample.

Use with pages 36–37.

Read through the Modeled Instruction with students. Then read to them the sample item.

SAY **I can sketch a picture. *Sketch* means the same as — *take . . . draw . . . find*. Which word means the same as *sketch*? Mark your answer.**

Have students work items 1 through 8 as you read each sentence.

1 **Leap across the stream. To leap means to — *jump . . .walk . . . swim.***

2 **Joe tried to fling the net. To fling means to — *fold . . . throw . . . sink.***

3 **The baby was fussy. To be fussy means to be — *laughing . . . pretty . . . upset.***

4 **He lived in a cottage. A cottage is a — *small house . . . big house . . . old house.***

5 **Javier rode his usual path to school. If something is usual it is — *normal . . . long . . . busy.***

6 **The choir rehearsed for the show. To rehearse is to — *try out . . . practice. . . clap.***

7 **I was the original owner of the book. Original means the same as — *first . . . last . . . only.***

8 **Her grades improved by the end of the year. To improve means to — *fall . . . stay the same . . . get better.***

Use with page 38.

Read through the Modeled Instruction with students. Then read to them the sample story.

> **Summer was coming. Luis thought about what he would do on a perfect summer day. First, he would sleep until the birds woke him. After breakfast, he would spend the whole day riding his bike. That would be a great summer day.**

SAY **Now I will ask you a question about the story. What would wake Luis on his perfect summer day? Would it be — *an alarm clock . . . his mother calling. . .* or *the birds*? Find the picture that shows what would wake Luis.**

Read the story and the questions for items 1 and 2.

> **Even today, cowboys still work on ranches. They ride horses and use ropes to catch cows that get away. But the work of cowboys has changed. The cowboys do not need to travel across many states with the cows to take them to market. Now, the cows go by truck.**

1 **How do cows travel from state to state today? Do they go by — *airplane . . . truck . . .* or *walking in herds*?**

2 **What does a cowboy still need to do his job? Does he need — *a sheep . . . a shovel . . .* or *a horse*?**

Use with pages 39–41.

Read through the Modeled Instruction with students. Then read to them the sample story and the question.

> **Henry did not like his new baby sister. One day, when the baby was crying, Henry got really mad. He stuck out his tongue at her. The baby stopped crying. Then she laughed. His mother said he was the only one who could make her feel better. That made Henry feel great. He smiled at his new sister.**

SAY **How does Henry feel at the beginning of this story? Does he feel — *Happy . . . Scared . . .* or *Mad*?**

Read the story and the questions for items 1 through 3.

> **Jim wants to get a birthday gift for his father. He has only one dollar, though. He looks at the store. All he can buy is a candy bar or a pen. He does not think his father needs either one. He goes home and makes a card. In the card, he says he will let his father sleep late one Saturday. His father hugs him. He says it is the best birthday gift ever.**

1 **Jim does not think his father needs — *a book. . . a tie . . .* or *a pen.***

2 **Why does Jim's father like Jim's present to him? *It cost a lot of money. . . . Jim thought of the idea. . . . It is what he had asked for.***

3 **What does Jim make for his father? Does he make — *A picture . . . A cake. . .* or *A card*?**

Read the story and the questions for items 4 through 6.

You can make a paper bag puppet. First, you need a small brown paper bag. You need yarn. You need markers. You need glue. If you have anything like felt, you can use it, too. Plan your puppet. How will your puppet look? Draw the face on the top half of the bag. Draw a body on the rest of the bag. Glue on yarn for hair. Glue on felt for clothes. When everyone has a puppet, plan a play!

4 **What would be a good name for this story? Would it be — *"Coloring a Paper Bag". . . "Making a Mask" . . .* or *"Making a Puppet"*?**

5 **Which of these should you do first? Should you — *Draw a face . . . Get a bag, yarn, glue and markers . . .* or *Plan a play*?**

6 **What should you glue onto the face to make hair? Should you use — *Yarn. . . A brown bag . . .* or *Markers*?**

Read the story and the questions for items 7 through 10.

Susan and Dora liked to race. Sometimes Dora won. Sometimes Susan did. One day Dora decided she really wanted to win. She put her head down and began to run as fast as she could. She did not see a mail carrier coming. She ran into him and fell down. "You may be faster today," Susan said, "but I am smarter. I am still on my feet!"

7 **Who usually won when Susan and Dora raced? Was it — *Susan . . . Dora . . .* or *Sometimes Susan, and sometimes Dora*?**

8 **Who did Dora run into? Did she run into — *Susan . . . A mail carrier . . .* or *Dora's mom*?**

9 **Why did Susan say she is smarter than Dora? *Susan is still standing. . . . Susan gets better grades in school. . . . Susan reads a lot of books.***

10 **What lesson did Dora learn? *Winning isn't everything. . . . You always have to win. . . . Dora needs to stop running.***

Use with pages 42–43.

SAY **At the top of the page you see a group of people celebrating a birthday. Below the picture you see the words *came . . . birthday . . . part.* Which word tells about the picture?**

Continue in the same way for items 2 through 15.

Use with page 44.

SAY **At the top of the page you see the words *fingers . . . goldfish . . . crackers.* Which of these words has two words in it? Mark your answer.**

Continue in the same way for each group of words. Have students work items 2 through 5 as you read each group of words.

Use with page 45.

SAY **You see three words. Each word has a different ending. I will say one of the words and use it in a sentence. Then you will find the word. Mark next to *lifting.* The elephant was *lifting* a log. *Lifting.***

Have students work items 7 through 10 as you read each sentence.

7 **Mark next to *finishes.* He *finishes* one thing at a time. *Finishes.***

8 **Mark next to *closed.* She *closed* the door quietly. *Closed.***

9 **Mark next to *tightly.* They held the handle *tightly. Tightly.***

10 **Mark next to *stirring.* He was *stirring* the oatmeal. *Stirring.***

Use with page 46.

SAY **You see the words *who'd . . . who'll . . . who's.* Mark the space under the word that means *who is. Who is* going to take the bus? *Who is?***

Have students work items 12 through 15 as you read each sentence.

12 **Which one means *I will*? *I will* come tomorrow. *I will.***

13 **Which one means *it is*? *It is* too late for the movie. *It is.***

14 **Which one means *she will*? *She will* come again tomorrow. *She will.***

15 **Which one means *we are*? *We are* going to help you pack. *We are.***

Use with pages 47–48.

SAY **You see four words. The first word is *tease*. The letters *ea* in *tease* have a line under them. Which word has the same /ee/ sound as the letters *ea* in *tease*? Mark your answer.**

Have students work items 17 through 27 as you read each word.

Use with page 49.

SAY **You see two sentences. The sentences give facts or clues about one of the pictures. Then you see three pictures. Mark the picture that matches the information in the sentences. Work until you see the stop sign.**

Use with pages 50–51.

SAY **Look at the picture. Read the sentence. Choose the word that best completes the sentence to tell about the picture. Work until you see the stop sign.**

Use with pages 52–54.

SAY **You will read some short stories. Then you will answer questions about them. Mark the space for the answer you think is right. Work until you see the stop sign.**

Use with page 55.

SAY **I will say a word and use that word in a sentence. Look at the words by the number 1. Mark the correct way to spell the word that I say.**

1 ***Here*. *Here* is the book I was looking for. *Here*.**

2 ***Calling*. She heard her mother *calling* her home. *Calling*.**

3 ***Near*. The doorbell is *near* the door. *Near*.**

4 ***Bee*. A *bee* buzzed by the flower. *Bee*.**

5 ***Write*. Always *write* your name on your school work. *Write*.**

6 ***Pay*. I need to *pay* for my groceries. *Pay*.**

7 ***Quick*. The turtle was not *quick*. *Quick*.**

8 ***Thing*. The *thing* I like best about Mom is her jokes. *Thing*.**

Use with pages 56–57.

SAY **I will read a sentence. Each sentence has a part that is underlined. You will choose the best way to write the underlined part.**

Read the sentence for items 1 through 8, emphasizing the underlined part. Pause while students mark each answer.

Use with pages 58–59.

SAY **"The boy plays in his yard. With his wagon." How should these groups of words be written to make a complete and correct sentence? Should they be written *The boy plays in his yard with his wagon. . . . The boy playing in his yard with his wagon.* . . . or should it be written *The way it is*?**

Continue in the same way. Read items 10 through 14 as you did item 9.

Use with pages 60–61.

SAY **We will read a story together. Then we will read and answer questions about the story. Mark the space for the answer you think is best.**

Read the stories and the questions for items 15 through 18. Pause while students mark their answers.

Use with page 62.

SAY **Look at the words for number 19: *yard . . . forest . . . man*. Which word comes first in A-B-C order? Is it *yard, forest,* or *man*?**

Read items 20 through 24 as you did item 19.

Use with pages 63–64.

SAY **Listen as I say a sentence. Choose the word that means about the same thing as the word I use in a sentence.**

1 **I don't know whether we should go. Whether means the same as — *when . . . if . . . why.***

2 **We heard the baby wail. To wail means to — *cry . . . laugh . . . eat.***

3 **I have to pay a fine for an overdue library book. Overdue means — *late . . . early . . . on time.***

SAY **Listen as I read a story. Then listen to each question. Choose the picture that best answers each question about the story.**

Jody and her family were taking a walk. It was early spring. Everywhere there were spring flowers. Jody wanted to stop and look at every flower. By the end of an hour, Jody and her family had gone only one block!

4 **What season was it when Jody and her family took a walk? Was it — *winter . . . fall . . .* or *spring*?**

5 **Why did Jody and her family go only one block? *The baby was crying. . . . Jody looked at all the flowers. . . . The dog sniffed at every tree.***

SAY **Listen as I read a story. Then listen to each question. Choose the best answer for each question about the story.**

You can make a musical shaker. First, ask your mother for an old can. It should be the size of a soup can. Have your mother wash it. Then fill it part way with beans or rocks. Over the open end, put a piece of strong paper. Put a rubber band around the paper and the can. Now you have a shaker.

6 **What can you use to make the shaker? Can you use — *A soup can . . . A paper box . . .* or *A glass jar*?**

7 **What would be a good name for this story? *"How to Make a Shaker" . . . "Make a Can" . . . "Eating Soup."***

Read the story and the questions for items 8 and 9.

A girl sees a jar full of peanuts on the kitchen counter. She loves peanuts, so she puts her hand in the jar. She takes a big handful. She takes so many she cannot get her hand out. Her brother comes by. "Try taking fewer nuts," he tells her. She does. Then she can get her hand out and eat the peanuts.

8 **Why does the girl put her hand in the jar? *She wants to see if her hand will fit. . . . She wants peanuts. . . . She does it for fun.***

9 **What does the girl learn from what happened? *Eat a lot of peanuts. . . . Do not eat peanuts. . . . Do not be greedy.***

Use with pages 65–66.

SAY **At the top of the page you see a child and an adult doing laundry. Below the picture you see the words *wipe . . . wash . . . cloud*. Which word tells about the picture?**

B **Next you see the words *clothes . . . town . . . soup*. Which word tells about the picture?**

C **Then you see the words *close . . . heard . . .clean*. Which word also tells about the picture?**

Continue in the same way for Samples D through F and items 1 through 24.

Use with pages 67–69.

SAY **At the top of the page you see the words *pencil . . . anyone . . . longest*. Which of these words has two words in it? Mark your answer.**

Have students work items 1 through 4 on their own.

SAY **Find Sample B. You see three words. Each word has a different ending. I will say one of the words and use it in a sentence. Then you will find the word. Mark next to *cleaning*. Nan worked hard *cleaning* her room. *Cleaning*.**

Have students work items 5 through 8 as you read each sentence.

5 **Mark next to *waits*. He *waits* for the school bus. *Waits*.**

6 **Mark next to *clearly*. It is important to speak slowly and *clearly*. *Clearly*.**

7 **Mark next to *sailed*. The boat *sailed* away from the dock. *Sailed*.**

8 **Mark next to *slowest*. Which of these three animals runs *slowest*? *Slowest*.**

SAY **Find Sample C. You see the words *it's . . . hasn't . . . isn't*. Each of these words is a shortened form of two other words. Mark the space under the word that means *is not*. That book *is not* mine. *Is not*.**

Have students work items 9 through 12 as you read each sentence.

9 **Which one means *we have*? *We have* seen that movie. *We have*.**

10 **Which one means *she is*? *She is* in third grade. *She is*.**

11 **Which one means *were not*? The players knew they *were not* going to win. *Were not*.**

12 **Which one means *I would*? *I would* like to go with you. *I would*.**

SAY **Find Sample D. You see four words. The first word is *lamp*. The letter *l* in *lamp* has a line under it. Look at the three words in the row. Which word has the same /l/ sound as the letter *l* in *lamp*?**

Have students work Sample E and items 13 through 25 as you read each word.

Use with page 70.

SAY **You see two sentences and pictures of a sailboat, a doll, and a clock.**

The sentences give facts or clues about one of the pictures. Follow along as I read the sentences aloud: "It has hands. It is a toy." Mark the picture that matches the information in the sentences.

Have students work items 1 through 5 on their own.

Use with pages 71–72.

SAY **Look at the picture of a truck. Read the sentence. Choose the word that makes the sentence tell about the picture.**

Have students work items 6 through 17 on their own. Tell them to work until they see the stop sign.

Use with pages 73–76.

SAY **You will be reading some short stories. Then you will be answering questions about the stories. Look at the sample story. Read the story to yourself and answer the questions.**

Have students complete items 18 through 29 on their own.

Use with pages 77–78.

SAY **I will say a word and use the word in a sentence. Look at the three words in Sample A. Mark the correct way to spell the word that I say. *There*. Put the books over *there* on the shelf. *There*. Mark your answer.**

Have students work Sample B and items 1 through 30 as you read each sentence.

B **_Shout_. Please do not _shout_. _Shout_.**

1 **_Again_. Let's sing the song _again_. _Again_.**

2 **_Blue_. _Blue_ is my favorite color. _Blue_.**

3 **_Always_. I _always_ remember to walk my dog. _Always_.**

4 **_Any_. I haven't _any_ more food for the birds. _Any_.**

5 **_Trunk_. An elephant has a _trunk_. _Trunk_.**

6 **_Sorry_. I am _sorry_ that you missed the bus. _Sorry_.**

7 **_Hurt_. She fell down and _hurt_ her knee. _Hurt_.**

8 **_Care_. Jon will take _care_ of my cat this week. _Care_.**

9 **_Circus_. We saw lots of clowns at the _circus_. _Circus_.**

10 **_Fish_. A _fish_ makes a great pet. _Fish_.**

11 *Grew.* The sunflower plants *grew* very tall. *Grew.*

12 *Part.* Would you like a *part* in the class play? *Part.*

13 *Drink.* I would like some milk to *drink. Drink.*

14 *Page.* Look at the picture on this *page. Page.*

15 *Cake.* Dad baked a *cake* for my birthday. *Cake.*

16 *While.* Mom listens to me read *while* she cooks. *While.*

17 *Reach.* I can't *reach* things on the top shelf. *Reach.*

18 *Prize.* Who won first *prize*? *Prize.*

19 *Change.* I always *change* my clothes after school. *Change.*

20 *Cabin.* My granddad has a little *cabin* in the woods. *Cabin.*

21 *Call.* I will *call* you tonight. *Call.*

22 *Catch.* Can you *catch* a ball? *Catch.*

23 *Dishes.* Please put these *dishes* on the table. *Dishes.*

24 *Getting.* My aunt is *getting* a new car. *Getting.*

25 *Saved.* He *saved* money to buy a new bike. *Saved.*

26 *Toys.* I will help you put these *toys* away. *Toys.*

27 *Giving.* Are you *giving* him a present? *Giving.*

28 *Running.* Don't leave the water *running. Running.*

29 *Grapes.* This jam is made from *grapes. Grapes.*

30 *Sees.* He *sees* his grandmother every weekend. *Sees.*

Use with pages 79–80.

SAY **Listen carefully to the sentence for Sample A as I read it aloud. "My sister's name is helen." How should the underlined part be written? Should it be *Helen*? with a capital "H" and a question mark, like the first answer choice; *Helen.* with a capital "H" and a period, like the second answer choice; or should it be written *The way it is*? Mark your answer.**

Continue in the same way for Sample B and items 1 through 12.

Use with page 81.

SAY **Read the groups of words in the box as I read them aloud. "The turtle crawled. Across the road." How should these groups of words be written to make a complete and correct sentence? Should they be written *The turtle crawled across the road. . . . The turtle crawling across the road. . . .* or is this a complete and correct sentence *The way it is*? Mark your answer.**

Continue in the same way for Sample D and items 13 through 16.

Use with pages 82–83.

SAY **Look at the sample story in the box at the top of the page. Follow along as I read the story aloud.**

Ants are found almost everywhere. They live in groups called colonies. Some ant colonies can be found underground. Colonies can also be found inside trees, under logs, or in mounds of earth.

Now look at Question E. Read the question and the answer choices to yourself as I read them aloud. Which of these would go *best* after the last sentence? *Most ants are black, brown, or red. . . . An ant's body has three main parts. . . . Colonies of ants can even make nests from tree leaves.* Mark your answer.

Continue in the same way for Sample E and items 17 through 22.

Use with page 84.

SAY **Look at the words in the box: *bed . . . lamp . . . radio.* Which word comes first in alphabetical (A-B-C) order? Is it *bed, lamp,* or *radio*? Mark the space next to your answer.**

Have students complete items 23 through 28 as you read each group of words.

Use with page 85.

SAY **I will read a sentence. Then I will say a word from the sentence and the three words that are written in your booklet. Choose the word that means the same as the word from the sentence. I try not to shove anyone in line. To shove means to — *push . . . talk to . . . touch.* Which word means the same as *shove*? Mark the space next to your answer.**

Have students complete items 1 through 10 as you read each sentence.

1 **Can you repair my bike? To repair means to — *ride . . .fix . . . see.***

2 **Grasp the bar. To grasp is to — *hold . . .throw . . . put.***

3 **Did you make an error? An error is the same as a — *drawing . . . meal . . . mistake.***

4 **Did you locate your homework? To locate is to — *do . . . find . . .give.***

5 **I take a stroll with my dog. A stroll means the same as a — *walk . . . run . . . bath.***

6 **That fox is untamed. *Untamed* means the same as — *hungry . . . wild . . . sleeping.***

7 **I am feeling healthy today. Healthy means the same as — *sad . . . happy . . . well.***

8 **I ate the entire sandwich. Entire means the same as — *half . . . whole . . . hot.***

9 **My mother likes to relax after work. To relax means to — *rest . . . cook . . . play.***

10 **Please forgive me. Forgive means — *talk to . . . excuse . . . sing to.***

Use with page 86.

SAY **Listen as I read a story. Then listen to each question. Choose the picture that best answers each question about the story.**

> **Places called mints make the coins we use every day. They are busy places. People who work in mints use tons of copper, silver, and other metals to make the coins. You can tell when you have a coin that was just made because it is shiny.**

B **Which picture shows what mints make? Do mints make — *coins . . . paper money* . . . or *candy*?**

C **Which person works in a mint? Would the person — *work at a store . . . build a house* . . . or *work with metal*? Mark your answer.**

Read the story and the questions for items 11 and 12.

> **Here's how you make a s'more. They are called s'mores because after you try them, you want some more. First, you need a campfire. You also need a stick, a marshmallow, graham crackers, and chocolate squares. Put the chocolate on a graham cracker. Then toast the marshmallow. Place the roasted marshmallow on the chocolate. Put the other graham cracker on the marshmallow. You have a s'more!**

11 **Which of these do you need to make a s'more? Do you need — *an oven . . . a pan on the stove* . . .or *a campfire*?**

12 **What does a s'more look like? Does it look like — *a sandwich . . . a pile of foods* . . . or *an apple*?**

Read the story and the question for items 13 and 14.

People have not always had books. Long before there were books, thousands of years ago, people wrote on tablets of clay. These were very thick pages made of clay. Then people learned how to make paper. People sat and wrote out every book, one by one. Today, we have huge machines called printing presses. They can make thousands of books. That is why we have so many more books today than in ancient days.

13 **Which of these was the way people first made books? *They used printing presses to create books like we have today. . . . They wrote out every book. . . . They wrote on tablets of clay.***

14 **Before printing presses, how did people make books? Did they use — *an old press . . . a computer . . .* or *pen and paper*?**

Read the story and the questions for items 15 and 16.

One day the class snake got loose. Everyone began to run. Ms. Jacon told us not to be scared. She said that the snake would be more frightened then we were. She said it was not poisonous. Then someone saw the snake poke its head into the room. No one moved. The snake moved slowly into the room. It saw its cage. The snake moved right in there, and Ms. Jacon shut the cage door. Even though we knew the snake was not dangerous, we were glad the snake was home.

15 **Where was the snake at the end of the story? Was it — *in Ms. Jacon's arms . . . in its cage . . .* or *on the floor*?**

16 **How did the children feel at the end of the story? Did they feel — *scared . . . happy . . .* or *angry*?**

Use with pages 87–88.

Read the story and the questions for the sample items.

Once again, Katy had forgotten to bring her homework to school, even though she had done it. Her teacher was mad at her. Katy tried to think where her homework was. Yesterday, right after school, she had done her homework on the table while she ate a peanut butter sandwich. She played with her dog Lindy. Then she went to play with her friend Nelia. Katy thought about what she had done. She thought the homework must be on the table. When she got home, she looked at the table. No homework was there. Katy sat down and sighed. Then she heard a sound. Under the table was Lindy. She was licking peanut butter off of Katy's homework.

D **Who is Nelia? Is she — *Katy's dog . . . Katy's friend . . .* or *Katy's sister*? Mark your answer.**

E **A good title for this story would be — *"Katy's Pet Cat" . . "Katy's Lost Homework" . . . or "Katy and Nelia"*? Mark your answer.**

SAY **Find the section with numbers 17 through 18 in it. Listen closely as I ask you more questions about the story.**

17 **Why was this story written? *To give directions . . . To tell a story . . . To tell how to do a job.***

18 **What do you think Katy will learn from what happened? Will she learn to — *trust her dog . . . eat snacks . . .* or *take better care of her homework*?**

Read the story and the questions for items 19 through 21.

Artists in Japan make art from paper. They have done this for hundreds of years. It is called origami. The artists fold paper. When they are done, the paper may look like animals. It may just be lovely shapes. Some origami is very easy. Some is very hard to do. About 50 years ago, a man found a way to show how to make the folds. After that, people started doing origami all over the world.

19 **What is origami? Is it — *Artists who fold paper . . . The art of folding paper . . .* or A *Japanese food*?**

20 **Which of these is true of origami? *It is very old. . . . You use metal to do it. . . . No one can do it today.***

21 **What happened after a man showed how to make the folds? *No one did origami. . . . More people started to do origami. . . . A man made origami animals.***

Read the story and the questions for items 22 and 23.

Jenny's birthday was coming. She should be happy, but she was sad. No one seemed to care. No one asked what she wanted to do for her birthday. No one asked what kind of cake she wanted. Jenny just knew they had all forgotten. On her birthday, no one said a word. After school, Jenny went up to her room and cried. Then her mother called. "Jenny," she said, "please come down and practice the piano.

"All right," said Jenny. She was still sniffling. She went downstairs. There, she saw her whole family. Her friends were there, too.

"Surprise!" they all yelled. It would be a happy birthday after all, Jenny thought.

22 **How did Jenny feel at the end of this story? Did she feel — *Sad . . . Mad . . . Happy*?**

23 **Why did Jenny's mother really want her to come downstairs? *To come to the party . . . To practice the piano . . . To do her homework.***

Read the story and the questions for items 24 and 25.

Sam was going with his older brother Jason to their aunt's house. "Sam," his mother said, "I'm going to tell you and Jason the way. Pay attention. First, turn left on Elm. That is right at the end of this block. Then go three blocks. You will see a small house on Elm with the number 233. That is your Aunt Gail's house. Do you remember? Take one turn, and then go three blocks to 233 Elm."

24 **What did you just listen to? Did you listen to — *A story . . . A recipe . . .* or *Directions*?**

25 **Who lives at 233 Elm? Is it — *Jason . . . Sam . . .* or *Aunt Gail*?**

Read the story and the questions for items 26 and 27.

Maria was looking at pictures. She saw one of a tiny baby with big brown eyes. "Mom!" Maria said. "She's so cute! Who is she?"

"Someone you know," her mother said.

"Is it Dawn?" Dawn was Maria's sister.

"No," said her mother. "But now, look at this picture." Her mother took out another baby picture. This baby looked just like the first baby!

"Is this the same baby?" Maria asked.

"No," her mother said. "The first baby picture is you. The second one is me. Don't we look alike?"

"We do!" Maria said. Then she looked at her mother. "Am I going to look like you some day?" she asked. Her mother laughed.

"Maybe, Maria, maybe," she said.

26 **Who is the baby in the first picture? Is it — *Maria . . . Dawn . . .* or *Maria's mother*?**

27 **What would be a good title for this story? *"Baby Pictures" . . . "Maria's Eyes" . . . "Maria's Sister."***

Read the story and the questions for items 28 through 30.

In 1848, the news spread around the world. There was gold in California! A man named James Marshall had found the gold. He wanted to keep it secret, but people found out. People found gold nuggets in streams. They dug mines and found gold. Before long, 200,000 people were looking for gold. Many of them found it. The California gold rush made some people very rich.

28 **In what state was the Gold Rush of 1848? Was it in — *Alaska . . . Nevada . . .* or *California*?**

29 **What did James Marshall do? Did he — *Tell everyone about the gold . . . Find the gold . . .* or *Govern the state of California.***

30 **Why did so many people go to California in 1848? *They followed their families. . . . They wanted to see the gold. . . . They wanted to get rich.***

Student's Name ______________________________

Teacher's Name ______________________________

SUBTESTS	Date/Score Modeled Instruction	Date/Score Guided Practice	Date/Score Practice Test
Word Reading			
Word Study Skills 1. structural analysis (compounds, inflections, contractions) 2. phonetic analysis—consonants (single, clusters, digraphs) 3. phonetic analysis—vowels (short, long, other)			
Reading Comprehension 1. narrative 2. expository 3. functional			
Spelling 1. sight words 2. phonetic principles (consonant sounds, vowel sounds) 3. structural principles (inflections)			
Language 1. mechanics (capitalization, punctuation, usage) 2. expression (sentence structure, content, organization) 3. A-B-C order			
Listening 1. vocabulary 2. comprehension			

Strengths/Areas for Improvement: ______________________________

Using the Introduction to the Student Book

Becoming familiar with the test-taking experience can help students do their best on standardized tests. The Introduction provides guidance for acquainting your students with standardized tests, so that they can spend less time figuring out what they are supposed to do and more time showing what they know. Before students begin the work on page 9, guide them through the Introduction on pages 3–8.

Use with page 3.

Read the letter to students. Ask them to describe how the tortoise and the hare are different. Have them tell some other things that the tortoise and the hare might do.

Use with page 4.

Have students follow along as you read the paragraph in dark type and the tortoise's tips. Ask students to tell why being prepared will help them do better on a test.

Use with page 5.

Tell students that answer marking is an important test-taking skill. Explain to students that sometimes a machine will grade their tests, and they must mark each answer in the way that the machine will recognize it. Read the paragraph in dark type to students. Then help them complete the items on the page.

Use with page 6.

Describe to students what they should do when they see a sample item, a go on arrow, and a stop sign on a test. Then read the paragraph in dark type. Help students complete the items on the page.

Use with page 7.

Have students follow along as you read the paragraph in dark type. Show students how to do item 1. Then have them complete the items on the page.

Use with page 8.

Read the checklist to students, and have them check the boxes to show what they will do when they take a test.

Standardized Test Preparation Book for Reading and Language Arts

Grade 1

Orlando Boston Dallas Chicago San Diego

Visit *The Learning Site!*
www.harcourtschool.com

Printed in the United States of America

ISBN 0-15-321227-6

9 073 2007 2006 2005

Contents

Name ____

Dear Student,

Once a year the children in your school take a special test. This test helps the teachers and the principal know what you are learning.

Taking the test is easier when you know how. This book will help you learn how. It will give you practice listening carefully, reading carefully, and following directions.

Take some hints from the tortoise and the hare. The tortoise reads carefully and chooses the best answers. The hare is careless and makes mistakes. Will you be like the tortoise or the hare?

- ✔ LISTEN carefully.
- ✔ READ carefully.
- ✔ CHOOSE the best answer.
- ✔ MARK answer choices carefully.
- ✔ CHECK your work.

Name ______________________________

The tortoise is always prepared and ready to pay attention to the teacher. Think about how you can be ready for a test. Then read the tortoise's tips below.

Tips for Listening

1. Sit quietly.
2. Look at the speaker.
3. Listen for directions.
4. Do not pay attention to other students.
5. Listen to important information.

Tips for Taking a Test

1. Sit up straight in your chair.
2. Keep your eyes on the teacher or on the test booklet.
3. Have your sharpened pencils ready.

Name ___________________________________

You should mark answer choices carefully when you take a test. The tortoise fills each circle completely. The hare is messy and marks outside the circle. Follow the directions for each item below. Mark your answers as the tortoise would.

1 Mark the answer circle on the left.

2 Mark the answer circle at the top.

3 Mark the answer circle for the picture of the hare.

4 Mark the answer circle for the picture of the tortoise.

Name ______________________________

You will see some important words when you take tests. These words tell you what to do. Look at the words and pictures. Then answer the questions. Remember to mark each answer choice as the tortoise would.

	SAMPLE	GO ON	STOP
1 What word or words tell you to keep working?	○	●	○
2 What word or words tell you the teacher will show you how to do an item?	●	○	○
3 What word or words tell you to put your pencil down?	○	○	●

Name ______________________________

Sometimes important information on a test has a line under it. Sometimes the information is in a box. The hare gets questions wrong because he does not pay attention to the important information. Mark the answer circle that shows the important information from each question below.

1. **m<u>u</u>g**

   m ○ u ● g ○

2. **b<u>oa</u>t**

   b ○ oa ● t ○

3. **A thing that is <u>untied</u> is ____________.**

   that is ○ untied ● thing ○

4. **Which one tells something Kenny did <u>not</u> do?**

   Kenny ○ tells ○ not ●

5. **What is the <u>best</u> title for this story?**

   best ● title ○ story ○

6. **I am ready to <u>play.</u>**

   I ○ am ○ play. ●

Fill in the checklist to show what you will do when you take a test.

I will

- ❒ listen carefully.
- ❒ read carefully.
- ❒ follow directions.
- ❒ mark answers carefully.
- ❒ begin where told.
- ❒ begin when told.
- ❒ stop when told.
- ❒ guess carefully.
- ❒ check my answers.
- ❒ pay attention only to the teacher and the test.
- ❒ do the best I can.

____

Name

Name ____________________ 

Modeled Instruction: Word Reading

You will look at some pictures. Then you will choose words that tell about the pictures.

Word Reading When you look at a picture, think about what is happening. Look for details that tell who, what, where, when, and why.

Test-Taking Tip Look at each word carefully. Some words may begin with the same sound. Some words may end with the same sound. Only one word in each row is correct.

Look at the Sample. Ask yourself what is going on in the picture. Then read the words in each row. You should mark the spaces for telephone, talk and street.

SAMPLE

store ○	telephone ●	party ○
talk ●	party ○	walk ○
hose ○	card ○	street ●

GO ON

 Name

Practice

Word Reading

1. spot ○ sip ○ spin ●
2. skates ● fall ○ listen ○
3. its ○ ice ● idea ○

Tip
The words spot and spin begin with the same sounds. Look carefully at the rest of each word before you mark your answer.

4. reading ● letter ○ dinner ○
5. start ○ chair ● chain ○
6. boot ○ write ○ book ●

Tip
Take a careful look at the words boot and book. Ask yourself how these words are alike and different. Pay special attention to the letter at the end before you mark your answer.

GO ON

Name

7	winner ○	fire ○	windy ●
8	king ○	kites ●	wink ○
9	fly ●	tree ○	birds ○

Tip

The picture shows a boy washing a truck. Choose the words that tell about the picture.

10	wash ●	watch ○	bike ○
11	close ○	hose ●	home ○
12	truck ●	table ○	drop ○
13	yarn ○	yard ●	learn ○
14	clap ○	grab ○	grass ●
15	cut ●	cute ○	glass ○

Tip

The words cut and cute look alike, and the word glass looks a lot like grass. Don't be fooled by words that look alike.

STOP

 Name

Modeled Instruction: Word Study Skills

You will be reading groups of words. Then you will choose the compound word in each group of words.

Compound Words A compound word is formed when two words are joined to make a new word.

Test-Taking Tip A word part is not the same as a word. The answer you choose should be made up of two smaller words.

Read the Sample. Look carefully at each word. Which word is made up of two smaller words? The words birth and day make up the longer word birthday. You should mark the space for birthday.

SAMPLE

- ○ running
- ● birthday
- ○ landed

Practice

Word Study Skills

1
- ○ monkey
- ○ garden
- ● everyone

2
- ○ picnic
- ○ rabbit
- ● snowstorm

Tip

Look again at the answer you chose. What are the two smaller words? Try to use each one in a sentence.

GO ON

Name 

3
- ○ better
- ● football
- ○ unhappy

4
- ○ talking
- ○ hammer
- ● airplane

Tip

Draw a line between the two words in the compound word. Make sure you have chosen the correct answer.

5
- ● sunrise
- ○ played
- ○ writer

6
- ○ invite
- ○ swimmer
- ● doorbell

Tip

You may see at least one smaller word in each answer choice. Pick the one that has two smaller words.

7
- ○ movie
- ● anything
- ○ water

8
- ● something
- ○ paper
- ○ return

STOP

Name

Modeled Instruction: Word Study Skills

You will listen carefully to your teacher to answer the questions for this part of the test.

Word Endings A word ending changes the meaning of a word. Your teacher will say a word and then use the word in a sentence. You will mark the space for the word your teacher says.

Test-Taking Tip Listen to the word ending that your teacher says. Think about how to spell the word ending before you look at the answer choices.

Listen to the Sample. Say each of the answer choices to yourself. You should mark the space for singer because that is the word your teacher said.

SAMPLE

- ○ singing
- ○ sings
- ● singer

Practice

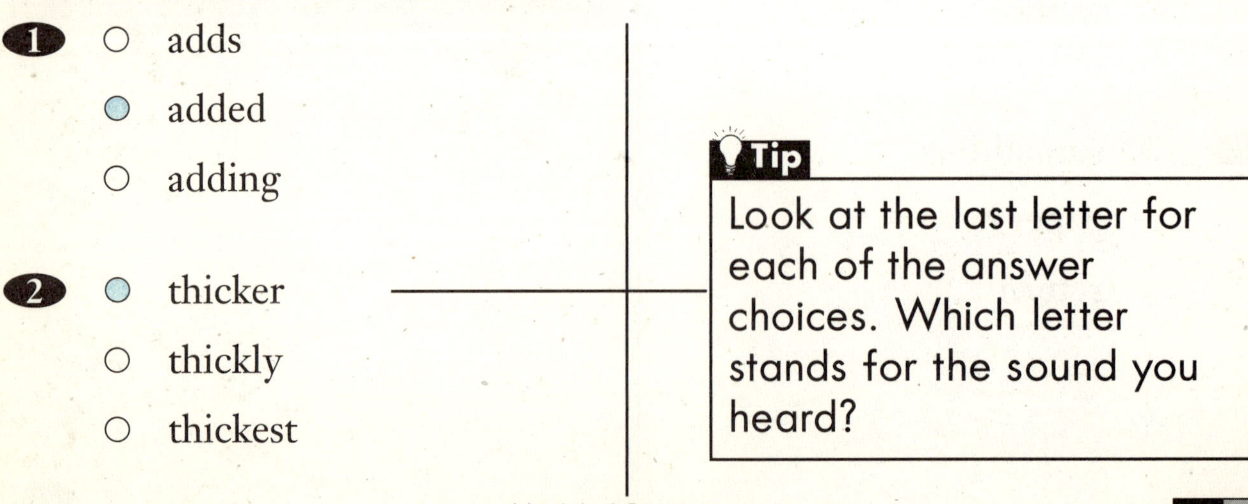

Name

3
- ○ thanking
- ○ thanks
- ○ thanked

4
- ○ digs
- ○ digging
- ○ digger

5
- ○ nicely
- ○ nicer
- ○ nicest

Tip Sound out each of the answer choices. Then choose the word that your teacher said.

6
- ○ walking
- ○ walked
- ○ walks

7
- ○ louder
- ○ loudly
- ○ loudest

Tip You may try to spell the word ending before you look at the answer choices.

8
- ○ shortly
- ○ shortest
- ○ shorter

STOP

 Name

Modeled Instruction: Word Study Skills

Joined Words Some words can be joined to make a contraction. Every contraction has an apostrophe that shows where a letter or letters are missing. Your teacher will say two words and then use the words in a sentence. You will choose the contraction that means the same as the two words your teacher says.

Test-Taking Tip You have picked the right answer if you can take out the apostrophe and replace it with the missing letter or letters.

Listen to the Sample. Say each of the answer choices to yourself. You should mark the space for you'd. You would and you'd have the same meaning.

SAMPLE

you're	you'd	you'll
○	●	○

Practice

Word Study Skills

1	she's ○	she'd ●	she'll ○
2	we're ●	we'd ○	we'll ○
3	won't ○	who'd ○	who's ●
4	isn't ○	it's ●	I'm ○

Tip
Look at each word. Which one has an ending that is almost the same as we are?

STOP

Name ______________________________ 

Modeled Instruction: Word Study Skills

Letter Sounds You will show how well you know letter sounds. You will read a word that has a letter or letters underlined. Then you will pick the word with the same sound as the underlined letters.

Test-Taking Tip Make sure you look at the underlined letters.

Read the Sample. Look at the word in dark type. The letter t has a line under it. You should mark the space for mat. Tool and mat have the same t sound.

SAMPLE

tool

mat	pan	hop
●	○	○

Practice

Word Study Skills

1 **mop**

man	horn	pot
●	○	○

Tip

Be careful. Mop and pot have the same p sound, but you are looking for a word with the m sound.

2 **song**

cap	note	miss
○	○	●

3 **swing**

sing	wind	swan
○	○	●

GO ON

Name

4 mask

mast ○ skip ○ kiss ○

5 tree

right ○ tar ○ trip ○

6 flag

float ○ legs ○ fast ○

7 grass

kiss ○ grape ○ map ○

8 went

weak ○ best ○ want ○

9 hunt

huge ○ think ○ luck ○

Tip

Th sk sound may not be at the end of the word like in mask.

Tip

Remember that you are looking for the fl sound, not the f sound.

Tip

Don't be fooled by words that look almost the same. Remember to listen for the sound of the underlined letter.

GO ON

Name ______________________________ 

10 **head**

edge ● heat ○ her ○

11 **milk**

pill ● call ○ mile ○

12 **gate**

paste ● latch ○ barn ○

13 **roast**

lodge ○ post ● phone ○

14 **hold**

how ○ own ● song ○

15 **my**

may ○ inch ○ sign ●

Tip

Sometimes the same letters stand for a different sound. The ea in head does not sound the same as the ea in heat.

Tip

Say each word to yourself before you mark an answer. The answer might surprise you.

STOP

Name

Modeled Instruction: Reading Comprehension

Sentences You will read sentences and look at pictures. The sentences give facts or clues about the correct answer.

Test-Taking Tip Think about the sentences and the pictures. Ask yourself questions about the sentences.

Read the Sample. Which thing can you both read and carry? You should mark the space for the picture of the book.

Practice

Reading Comprehension

1 It goes on the table. You can drink from it.

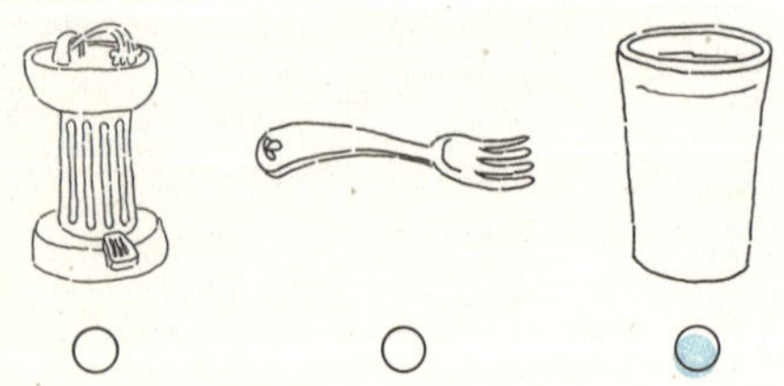

2 It is a machine. It can roll.

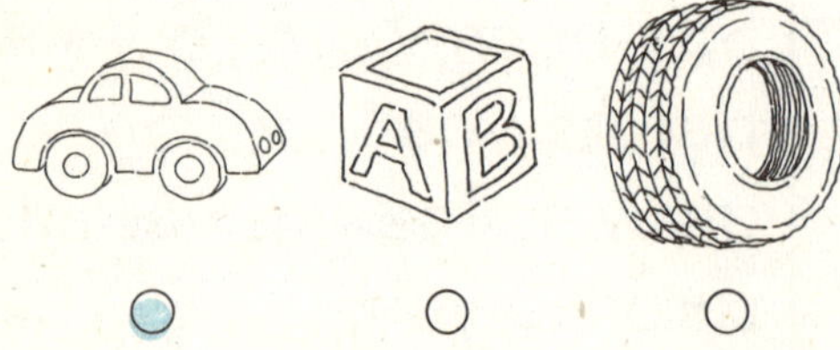

Tip

Both the car and tire and can roll. Which picture shows a machine that can roll?

STOP

Name ______________________________

Modeled Instruction: Reading Comprehension

You will look at a picture and answer questions about it.

Picture Clues Pictures give information and help you understand what you read.

Test-Taking Tip Look carefully at the picture. Think to yourself about what is in the picture.

Read the Sample. Look at the picture, and read the sentence. Choose the word that best tells about the picture. Only the word horse names the picture.

SAMPLE

Here is a

cow ○ horse ○ horn. ○

Practice

Reading Comprehension

1 **The family is**

cooking ○ working ○ reading. ○

Name

2 **The day is very**

hop ○ hot ● cool. ○

> **Tip**
> Don't be fooled by words that look alike.

3 **The children are at the**

beach ● bench ○ boat. ○

4 **The children buy cold**

cookies ○ eggs ○ drinks. ●

> **Tip**
> Think about what you would like to buy on a sunny day.

STOP

Name ____________________

Modeled Instruction: Reading Comprehension

You will read a story. Then you will answer some questions about it.

Story When you read a story, think about what happens. Look for details that tell who, what, where, when, and why.

Test-Taking Tip Ask yourself what kind of detail each question is asking about.

Read the Sample. You can tell by reading the question that you should look for a pet that Luz did not see. Look back at the story to check your answer.

SAMPLE

Luz's New Pet

Luz and Mom went to the pet shop. They looked at fish, rabbits, and kittens. Luz picked out a rabbit and a cage. Mom got a book about the new pet.

Luz did not look at

- ○ kittens
- ○ fish
- ● birds.

GO ON

Name ______________________

Practice

Reading Comprehension

Chipmunk Forgets

Chipmunk was walking in the woods. He was looking for nuts. His basket was almost full. Just then, Owl and Beaver came down the path. They were carrying flowers and a cake.

"Hello, Chipmunk," said Owl. "Are you ready to go to Squirrel's party? I see you have your present."

"Oh, my!" said Chipmunk. "I forgot all about the party. I'm glad I met you!"

"Let's go," said Beaver. "We don't want to be late."

Tip
What does Owl think Chipmunk will give Squirrel?

1 What did Chipmunk forget?

- ● Squirrel's party
- ○ A basket of nuts
- ○ Where Squirrel lives

2 What do you think Chipmunk will give to Squirrel?

- ○ Flowers
- ○ A birthday cake
- ● Nuts

Tip
If you don't remember what Chipmunk was carrying, look at the story again.

Name

Car Wash

Mrs. Lake's class is having a car wash. The students want to make money for a class trip.

Help our class earn money.
Get your car washed today.

car	**$3.00**
truck	**$5.00**
van	**$4.00**
bike	**50¢**

3 Why is the class having a car wash?

- ○ To help people
- ● To earn money
- ○ To clean up

4 How much will it cost to get a truck washed?

- ○ 50¢
- ● $5.00
- ○ $3.50

Tip

To answer this question, you need to go back and look carefully at the sign.

Name

Making Butter

Today you buy butter in a store. Years ago people had to make their own butter. The first thing they had to do was to pour cream in a big tub called a churn. This churn had a lid. It also had a long stick called a dasher. When the lid was on, someone moved the dasher up and down. Soon, bits of butter formed from the cream. When the butter was ready, it was washed and cooled. Then the butter was ready to eat.

5 What did you need to make butter?

- ○ Bread
- ○ Ice cream
- ● Cream

Tip

The story tells about only one of the answer choices. Pick the one you remember reading about.

6 In this story, the churn is used to

- ○ wash the butter
- ● turn cream into butter
- ○ hold the lid in place.

Tip

Go back to the story, and look for sentences that have the word <u>churn</u>. Then read this part of the story again to find out what a churn does.

STOP

Name ____________________

Modeled Instruction: Spelling

Spelling For this part of the test, your teacher will say a word and use the word in a sentence. You will pick the correct way to spell the word.

Test-Taking Tip Think about how you have seen each word spelled in other books.

Listen to the Sample. Think of how you would spell the word. Then look at the answer choices. You should mark the space for <u>said</u>.

SAMPLE

sed	said	siad
○	●	○

Practice

Spelling

1	duz ○	dos ○	does ●
2	when ●	wen ○	whun ○

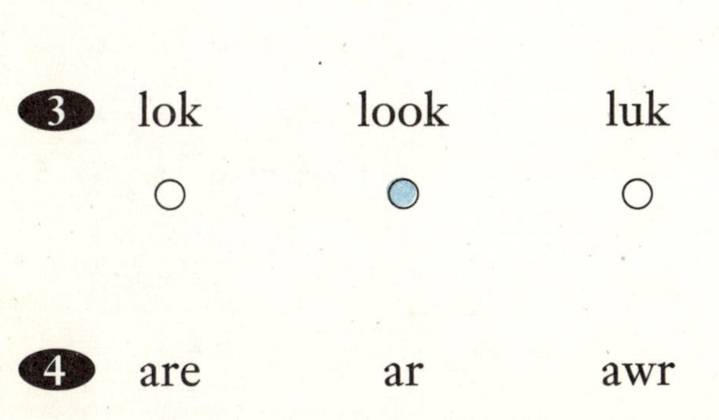

3	lok ○	look ●	luk ○
4	are ●	ar ○	awr ○

Tip

Pick a word that rhymes with the word your teacher said. How is the word spelled? Change the first letter to an <u>l</u> to find the correct answer.

GO ON

Name

5	hapy ○	happy ○	happey ○
6	pitch ○	pith ○	pitsh ○
7	kno ○	knoo ○	know ○
8	ligt ○	light ○	lite ○
9	dich ○	ditsh ○	dish ○
10	city ○	sity ○	citty ○
11	wun ○	one ○	whon ○
12	tyme ○	time ○	tim ○

Tip

Remember that some words have silent letters. What is the silent letter in this word?

Tip

Listen carefully to the ending sound in this word. Think about the letters that stand for the sound.

STOP

Name ______________________ 

Modeled Instruction: Language

You will read some sentences. Each sentence has an underlined part. You will choose the best way to write the underlined part.

Mechanics You will be asked to decide if a sentence is written the correct way. Some questions are about capital letters and end marks. Other questions are about words.

Test-Taking Tip Read the whole sentence. If you are sure that the underlined part is correct, mark The way it is.

Read the Sample. Ask yourself what kind of sentence it is. It is an asking sentence. It should end with a question mark. Mark the first space.

SAMPLE

Where is my book.

- ● book?
- ○ Book!
- ○ The way it is

Practice

Language

1 **My birthday is in may.**

- ○ may?
- ● May.
- ○ The way it is

Tip

Remember that days of the week and months of the year always begin with a capital letter.

GO ON

Name

2 **Watch out! That pan is very hot?**

- ● hot!
- ○ Hot.
- ○ The way it is

Tip
To decide if a sentence should end with a period or an exclamation point, think of how you would say the sentence.

3 **Dad will be home on thursday.**

- ○ thursday!
- ● Thursday.
- ○ The way it is

4 **The girl run across the yard.**

- ● runs
- ○ are running
- ○ The way it is

Tip
Make sure the naming part and telling part of the sentence go together.

5 **She thinked about her answer for a long time.**

- ○ think
- ● thought
- ○ The way it is

STOP

Name ______________________________

Modeled Instruction: Language

You will read groups of words. Then you will decide if the words make a complete sentence.

Expression Remember that every sentence has a naming part and a telling part.

Test-Taking Tip Say to yourself the words in each box. Choose the answer that is a complete thought.

Read the Sample. The words in the box are split into two groups. The first part is a complete sentence. At the cat is not a complete sentence. You should mark the first answer choice, because it is a complete thought.

SAMPLE

The dog barked. At the cat.

- ● The dog barked at the cat.
- ○ The dog barking at the cat.
- ○ The way it is

Practice

Language

1

Tim went to the store. After lunch.

- ○ Tim went. To the store after lunch.
- ● Tim went to the store after lunch.
- ○ The way it is

Tip

Join the words to make one sentence.

GO ON

Name

2 **Mom wants us to help in the garden.**

- ○ Mom wants us to help. In the garden.
- ○ Mom wanting us to help in the garden.
- ● The way it is

Tip
A complete sentence has a naming part and a telling part. It must also make sense.

3 **My sister and I. We did the dishes.**

- ● My sister and I did the dishes.
- ○ My sister and I. Did the dishes.
- ○ The way it is

4 **Too many ants. Can ruin a picnic.**

- ○ Too many ants. They can ruin a picnic.
- ● Too many ants can ruin a picnic.
- ○ The way it is

Tip
Say each of the answer choices to yourself. Which one sounds correct?

STOP

Name ______________________________ 

Modeled Instruction: Language

Expression Follow along as your teacher reads the stories. You will answer questions about the stories. You may choose the best sentence to end a story. You may be asked to pick a sentence that does not go with the story.

Test-Taking Tip Pay attention to any underlined word in a question to help you choose the right answer.

Listen to the Sample. Jack decides not to ride his bike to school because it is raining. You need to pick the sentence that does <u>not</u> go with the story. The second answer choice is right, because the story does not tell about Jack's birthday. Mark the space for that answer.

SAMPLE

Jack went to the window and looked out. The sky was gray and it was raining. Soon the wind began to blow. "I guess I won't ride my bike to school," said Jack. Then he put on his raincoat.

Which of these would <u>not</u> go with the story?

- ○ Jack saw many big puddles outside.
- ● Jack got a bike for his birthday.
- ○ He looked for his umbrella and boots.

GO ON

Name

Practice

Language

Sometimes I help my dad cook. Last week we made vegetable soup. My job was to wash the vegetables. Dad's job was to cut them up. We both took turns stirring the soup as it cooked.

1 Which of these would not go with this story?

- ○ Dad tells me stories while we cook.
- ○ Mom likes to take me on bike rides in the park.
- ○ First, we went shopping for vegetables to put in the soup.

Tip

The story is about cooking with Dad. Do you think the sentence about bike rides with Mom goes with the story?

2 Which of these would go best after the last sentence?

- ○ It tasted so good I ate two big bowls.
- ○ I washed carrots, beans, and celery.
- ○ One time we made an apple pie.

Tip

This story tells about things in the order they happen. What would you do after you made soup?

STOP

Name ______________________________ 

Modeled Instruction: Language

A-B-C Order You will answer questions about A-B-C order. A-B-C order is the way letters and words are organized in a dictionary. Ball would come before mat because the letter b comes in the alphabet before the letter m.

Test-Taking Tip Sing the alphabet song to yourself if you can't remember where a letter comes in the alphabet.

Read the Sample. Look at the first letter of each word. Which of the words would come first in the dictionary? The right answer is dog because the letter d comes in the alphabet before m and t. Mark the space for dog.

SAMPLE

- ● dog
- ○ man
- ○ table

Practice

Language

1

- ○ wagon
- ● button
- ○ picnic

2

- ○ fish
- ○ frog
- ● farm

Tip

Remember to look at the second letter if the first letter in each word is the same.

STOP

Name ____________________

Modeled Instruction: Listening

For this part of the test, you need to listen carefully to sentences that are read to you.

Vocabulary Your teacher will read a sentence. Then you will pick a word that means the same thing as a word from the sentence.

Test-Taking Tip Look at your teacher while you listen to the sentence. Think about the meaning of the sentence.

Listen to the Sample. Find the word that means the same as sketch. Cross out any of the answer choices you know are not correct. You should mark the space for draw, because sketch and draw mean the same thing.

SAMPLE

- ○ take
- ● draw
- ○ put away

Practice

Listening

1
- ○ jump
- ○ walk
- ○ swim

2
- ○ fold
- ○ throw
- ○ sink

Tip
Choose the word that would not change the meaning of the sentence.

GO ON

Name

3 ○ laughing
○ pretty
○ upset

4 ○ small house
○ big house
○ old house

5 ○ normal
○ long
○ busy

6 ○ try out
○ practice
○ clap

Tip

Think about when you may have heard this word before. Choose the word that means the same as get ready.

7 ○ first
○ last
○ only

8 ○ fall
○ stay the same
○ get better

STOP

Name ______________________________

Modeled Instruction: Listening

Story You will listen to a story. Then you will answer questions about it. The answer choices for this part of the test are pictures.

Test-Taking Tip Try to make pictures in your mind as you listen to the story.

Listen to the Sample. One picture shows what would wake Luis. What is it? If you marked the picture of the birds, you are correct.

SAMPLE B

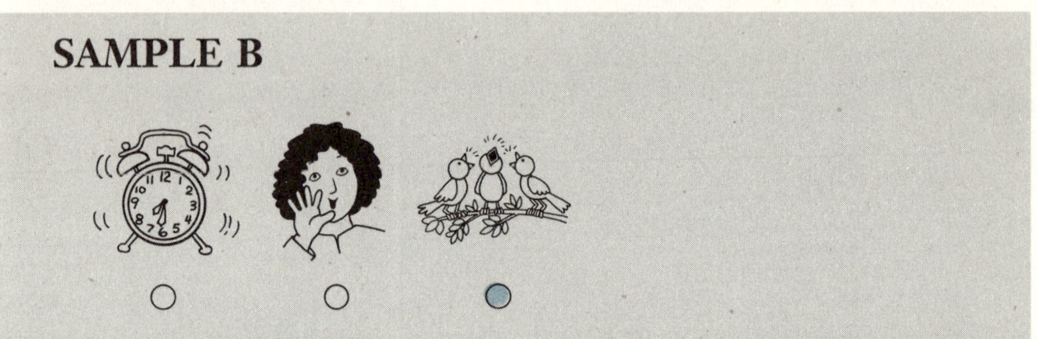

Practice

Listening

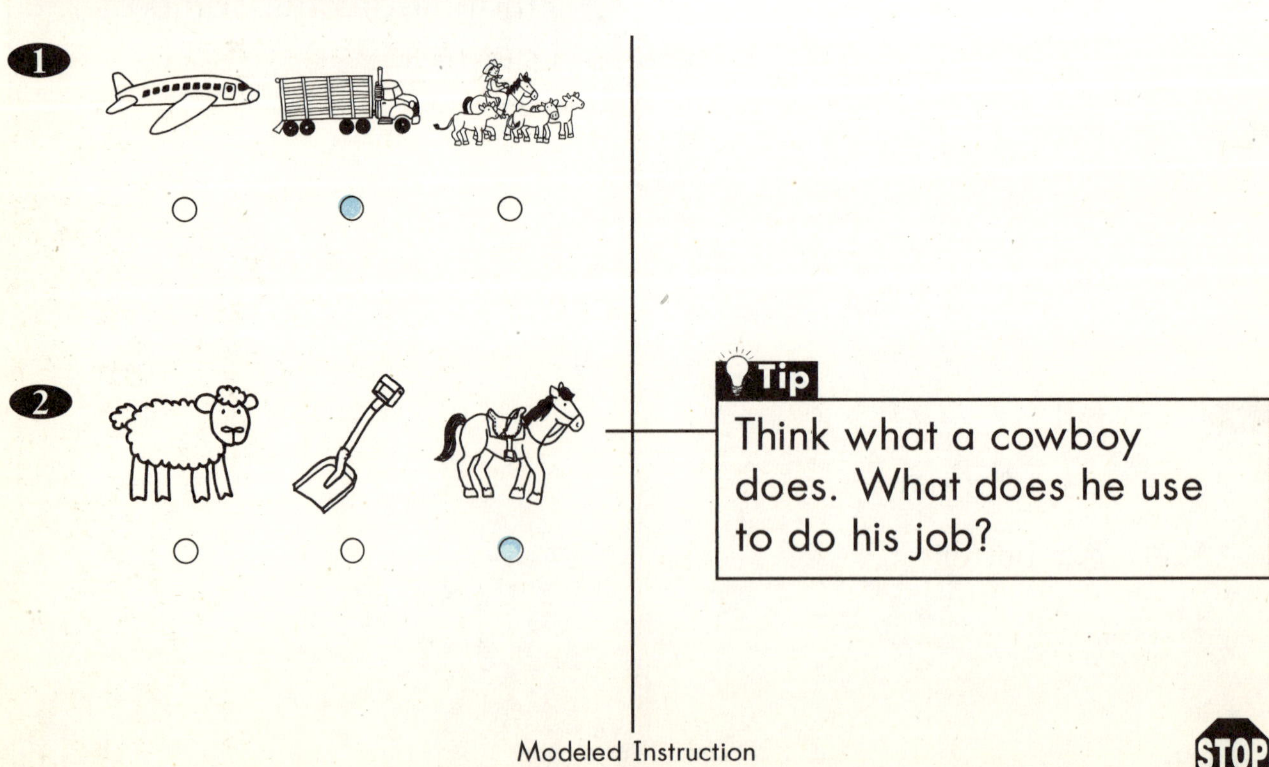

Tip

Think what a cowboy does. What does he use to do his job?

STOP

Name ____________________

Modeled Instruction: Listening

Stories You will listen to more stories for this part of the test. Then you will answer questions about each story. The questions may be about people in the story or things that happened in it.

Test-Taking Tip Think about the kind of story you hear. Is it telling you how to do something? Is the story telling you how someone feels?

Listen to the Sample. You should mark the answer choice that tells how Henry felt at the beginning of the story. Read the answer choices. Remember that Henry was happy at the end of the story. The story does not tell about Henry being scared. If you marked the space for mad, you are correct.

SAMPLE

- ○ Happy
- ○ Scared
- ● Mad

Practice

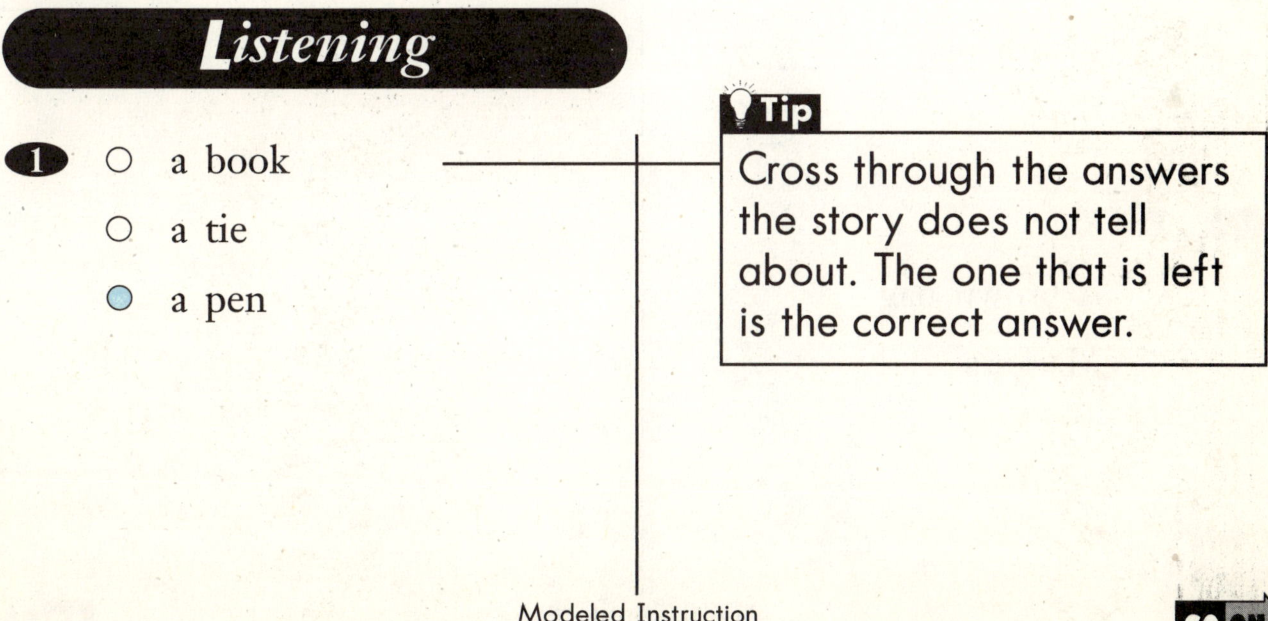

Name

2
- ○ It costs lots of money.
- ● Jim thought of the idea.
- ○ It is what he had asked for.

3
- ○ A picture
- ○ A cake
- ● A card

4
- ○ "Coloring a Paper Bag"
- ○ "Making a Mask"
- ● "Making a Puppet"

Tip

Think about the story. What is the main thing the story is telling?

5
- ○ Draw a face
- ● Get a bag, yarn, glue, and markers
- ○ Plan a play

Tip

Listen for words like <u>first</u>. They tell you in what order things happen.

6
- ● Yarn
- ○ A brown bag
- ○ Markers

GO ON

Name

7
- ○ Susan
- ○ Dora
- ● Sometimes Susan, and sometimes Dora

8
- ○ Susan
- ● A mail carrier
- ○ Dora's mom

9
- ● Susan is still standing.
- ○ Susan gets better grades in school.
- ○ Susan reads a lot of books.

Tip

Susan was not talking about grades. Why did she think she was smarter?

10
- ● Winning isn't everything.
- ○ You always have to win.
- ○ Dora needs to stop running.

Tip

If you are not sure of the answer, take away the ones you know are wrong. The one that is left is the correct answer.

STOP

 Name

Guided Practice

Word Reading

1. came ○ birthday ● part ○
2. party ● game ○ sink ○
3. fast ○ blocks ○ gifts ●

Tip
Look at the things on the table. What do you think the family is celebrating?

4. close ○ mess ● mark ○
5. tuck ○ truck ● bed ○
6. toys ● miss ○ clothes ○

Tip
Look carefully at the picture. Are the children picking up toys or clothes?

GO ON

Name

7 feet ○ bowl ● boil ○

8 fish ● flash ○ sales ○

9 fans ○ fist ○ swim ●

Tip Do fish have fans or fins? Don't be fooled by words that look alike.

10 tall ● hear ○ car ○

11 low ○ blocks ● blame ○

12 watching ○ paying ○ building ●

13 mall ○ tick ○ ice cream ●

14 cone ● come ○ snake ○

15 lake ○ mess ● colt ○

Tip Notice that something is dripping onto the girl's clothes.

STOP

 Name

Word Study Skills

1
- ○ fingers
- ● goldfish
- ○ crackers

Tip
Look for small words in each longer word. The answer you mark should have two small words.

2
- ○ splashing
- ○ pitcher
- ● airplane

3
- ● skateboard
- ○ unable
- ○ returned

Tip
The word parts un and re are often added to words to make new words. But these word parts are not words.

4
- ○ pleasant
- ● sandbox
- ○ sandwich

5
- ○ marches
- ● bluebird
- ○ pardon

STOP

Name ______________________________ 

6
- ○ lifting
- ○ lifts
- ○ lifted

7
- ○ finished
- ○ finishing
- ○ finishes

Tip Listen to the ending of the word your teacher says.

8
- ○ closed
- ○ closing
- ○ closes

9
- ○ tighter
- ○ tightly
- ○ tightest

10
- ○ stirring
- ○ stirs
- ○ stirred

Tip Sound out each of the answer choices. Then choose the word that your teacher said.

STOP

Name ______________________________

11 who'd who'll who's
- ○ who'd
- ○ who'll
- ● who's

12 I'll I'd I'm
- ● I'll
- ○ I'd
- ○ I'm

13 isn't it'll it's
- ○ isn't
- ○ it'll
- ● it's

Tip
This is a tricky word because it looks like the word <u>its</u>. The contraction <u>it's</u> can mean both <u>it is</u> and <u>it has</u>.

14 she's she'll she'd
- ○ she's
- ● she'll
- ○ she'd

15 we're we'd we'll
- ● we're
- ○ we'd
- ○ we'll

Tip
Think carefully about the two words <u>we are</u> used in the sentence. Which of these words has the same meaning?

STOP

Name

16 **tease**

thread ○ sneeze ● edge ○

17 **hay**

try ○ seat ○ stay ●

18 **city**

cat ○ race ● pack ○

19 **stem**

four ○ slip ○ fast ●

20 **judge**

must ● flute ○ huge ○

21 **thin**

mother ● tin ○ pinch ○

Tip

Say the word. Listen carefully for the soft sound of c, as in the words mice or cents.

Tip

Be sure to check both the beginnings and the ends of the words.

GO ON

 Name

22 **room**

floor ○ moon ● hook ○

23 **hike**

silk ○ ill ○ tie ●

24 **feed**

three ○ wife ● pony ○

25 **corn**

store ● low ○ word ○

Tip
Remember, the letter r changes some vowel sounds. Say each word. Listen for the vowel sound.

26 **snow**

smile ○ now ○ snake ●

27 **street**

sail ○ head ○ heat ●

Tip
Some vowel sounds have different spellings. Listen closely to the vowel sounds as you say the words.

STOP

Name

Reading Comprehension

1. **It flies.**
It has two legs.

○ ○ ●

2. **You use it to cook.**
You can pick it up.

○ ● ○

Tip

What is the one thing that you can cook with and pick up?

3. **It helps keep you dry.**
You can't wear it.

○ ● ○

Tip

All of these items may keep you dry. There is only one that you can't wear.

STOP

Name

4 **Here is a**

butterfly ○ frog ● fish. ○

5 **It can**

hop ● fly ○ whistle. ○

6 **The cats are**

eating ○ running ○ sleeping. ●

7 **They are both in a**

basket ● box ○ bucket ○

8 **in the**

bathroom ○ bedroom ● kitchen. ○

Tip

Look carefully at the picture to find out what the cats are doing.

Tip

Each word names a place in a home. Look at the picture for clues to help you choose the correct word.

GO ON

Name

9 **The Lees are**

playing ◉ eating ○ resting. ○

10 **They are tossing a**

bell ○ ball ◉ balloon ○

11 **in the**

garden ○ road ○ park. ◉

12 **The children watch a**

truck ○ band ◉ game. ○

13 **It is very**

fast ○ loud ◉ low. ○

Tip

Decide where this family is and what they are doing before you look at the answer choices.

Tip

Look at the children in the picture. What are they doing? What does this tell you?

STOP

Name

At the Pond

Danny and his dad took a walk to the pond. They saw a family of ducks. They also watched frogs and many tiny fish.

14 How did Danny and his dad get to the pond?

On foot ● By car ○ By bus ○

Tip Read the first sentence again to answer the question.

Sue and Jan

My name is Jan. Today a girl named Sue joined our class. She just moved here. I sat with her at lunch. We talked about animal stories. I think Sue and I will be good friends.

15 Jan seems very

busy ○ tired ○ nice. ●

16 You can tell Sue and Jan like

toys ○ animals ● plants. ○

Tip Think about what Sue and Jan talk about. This helps you to know what they like.

GO ON

Name

Making Pancakes

It's fun to make pancakes. Put some pancake mix in a big bowl. Then add milk and eggs. Stir the batter until the lumps in it are gone. Then drop spoonfuls of batter into a hot pan. Flip the pancakes when they turn brown.

17 **After adding eggs and milk, you must**

- ○ flip the pancakes
- ● stir the batter
- ○ drop spoonfuls in a pan.

18 **To make pancakes, you need pancake mix, milk, and**

eggs	sugar	salt.
●	○	○

Tip

Reread the first part of the story to find out what you need to make pancakes.

19 **You should stir the batter until**

- ○ the batter has lumps
- ○ the pan is hot
- ● the batter is smooth.

Tip

Think about how something looks when all the lumps are gone.

Name ____________________

Going Roller Skating

Nina is going to John's party at the Flying Wheels Skating Rink. John wrote down how to get there.

1. Go down Main Street, and cross the bridge.

2. Turn left. Go three blocks on Green Street. The rink is on the right beside the gas station.

20 **Nina should start at**

- ○ Bridge Street
- ● Main Street
- ○ Green Street.

Tip Choose the street that you read first.

21 **After she crosses the bridge, Nina should**

- ○ turn right
- ● turn left
- ○ turn around.

22 **The skating rink is near**

- ○ John's house
- ○ a bridge
- ● a gas station.

Tip Think of other words that have the same meaning as the word <u>near</u>.

STOP

Name

Spelling

1	heer ○	here ●	hir ○
2	calling ●	callng ○	caling ○
3	nere ○	neer ○	near ●
4	bea ○	bei ○	bee ●
5	rit ○	write ●	writ ○
6	pay ●	pai ○	pae ○
7	kwick ○	quick ●	quik ○
8	thind ○	thig ○	thing ●

Tip

Think about the two letters that stand for the beginning sound in this word. Remember that these letters always go together.

STOP

 Name

Language

1 **We went to the park last <u>sunday?</u>**

- ● Sunday.
- ○ sunday.
- ○ The way it is

Tip
Remember that days of the week begin with a capital letter.

2 **My sister <u>play</u> in the band.**

- ● plays
- ○ playing
- ○ The way it is

3 **Has the school bus <u>left yet?</u>**

- ○ left yet.
- ○ Left yet?
- ● The way it is

Tip
Ask yourself whether this is an asking sentence or a telling sentence.

4 **We <u>bakes</u> a cake yesterday.**

- ○ baking
- ● baked
- ○ The way it is

GO ON

Name

5 **I need a new pair of <u>Shoes?</u>**

- ○ shoes.
- ○ Shoes!
- ○ The way it is

6 **My brother's birthday is in <u>june.</u>**

- ○ june?
- ○ June.
- ○ The way it is

Tip

Remember that months of the year begin with a capital letter.

7 **Jane <u>bringed</u> her book of stickers to school.**

- ○ brought
- ○ bring
- ○ The way it is

Tip

Try saying each answer choice in the sentence. Which one sounds correct?

8 **Juan left the room to meet <u>Julie.</u>**

- ○ julie.
- ○ Julie,
- ○ The way it is

Tip

Think about how you write your name. Does it begin with a capital letter?

STOP

 Name

9

The boy plays in his yard. With his wagon.

- ○ The boy plays in his yard with his wagon.
- ○ The boy playing in his yard with his wagon.
- ○ The way it is

10

So many leaves are hard to rake!

- ○ So many leaves. Are hard to rake!
- ○ So many leaves. They're hard to rake!
- ○ The way it is

Tip

Remember that a sentence must tell a complete thought.

11

The children having a good time playing tag.

- ○ The children having a good time. Playing tag.
- ○ The children are having a good time playing tag.
- ○ The way it is

Tip

Some of the answer choices will look almost the same. Read each one carefully.

GO ON

Name

12 **Paula took a walk in the park. Yesterday afternoon.**

- ○ Paula took a walk in the park yesterday afternoon.
- ○ Paula took a walk. In the park yesterday afternoon.
- ○ The way it is

Tip

Try saying each group of words alone. Does each group tell a complete thought?

13 **We play tag. Every day after lunch.**

- ○ After lunch we play tag. Every day.
- ○ We play tag every day after lunch.
- ○ The way it is

Tip

Make sure that each sentence has a telling part.

14 **That painting on the wall. It is pretty.**

- ○ That painting on the wall is pretty.
- ○ That pretty painting on the wall.
- ○ The way it is

Tip

Read each sentence softly. Does it make sense?

STOP

Name

Nick's dad pulled into the car wash. Hoses squirted water at the car. Soapy brushes began to scrub. "This is fun," Nick said, as he watched from the backseat.

15 Why was this story written?

- ○ To tell about how the car got dirty
- ○ To tell about what kind of soap to use on a car
- ● To tell what it is like to get a car wash

Tip

Choose the answer that tells what the story is mostly about.

I love to sit around a campfire at night. It's fun to sing songs. It's also fun to also toast marshmallows over the coals.

16 Which of these would <u>not</u> go with this story?

- ○ While sitting, you can look up at the stars.
- ○ You can cook a midnight snack over the fire.
- ● We hiked five miles in the rain.

Tip

An underlined word in a question is very important.

Name ___

Bob had looked everywhere for his baseball glove. He checked under his bed. He looked in his toy box. Then he took everything out of his closet. He still could not find his glove.

17 **Which of these would go <u>best</u> after the last sentence?**

- ○ He found his old toy truck and a ball.
- ● He wondered if he had left the baseball glove at Joe's house.
- ○ He got the baseball glove as a birthday gift.

Tip

Try each answer choice as the last sentence to find out which one is best.

18 **Why was this story written?**

- ○ To tell about Bob's messy room
- ○ To tell how to use a baseball glove
- ● To tell how Bob looked for something

Tip

The story tells about a baseball glove, but it does not tell how to use a baseball glove.

STOP

Name

19
- ○ yard
- ● forest
- ○ man

20
- ● dog
- ○ rope
- ○ wall

Tip
Look at the first letter in each word. Then think about where each letter comes in the alphabet.

21
- ● baby
- ○ road
- ○ zoo

22
- ○ lunch
- ● come
- ○ house

23
- ○ soft
- ○ summer
- ● seat

Tip
If all the words begin with the same letter, you should look at the second letter in each word.

24
- ● penny
- ○ tag
- ○ wash

STOP

Name

Listening

1 ○ when
○ if
○ why

2 ○ cry
○ laugh
○ eat

3 ○ late
○ early
○ on time

4

○ ○ ○

5

Tip

Think of the sentence your teacher said. Say the sentence to yourself. Put in each answer word for *whether*. That will help you find the answer.

Tip

Think back to the story you just heard. There are clues that tell you what season it is.

GO ON

Name

6
- ○ A soup can
- ○ A paper box
- ○ A glass jar

7
- ○ "How to Make a Shaker"
- ○ "Make a Can"
- ○ "Eating Soup"

Tip
Choose the title that tells the main idea of the story.

8
- ○ She wants to see if her hand will fit.
- ○ She wants peanuts.
- ○ She does it for fun.

9
- ○ Eat a lot of peanuts.
- ○ Do not eat peanuts.
- ○ Do not be greedy.

Tip
Mark through the answers that do not make sense.

STOP

Name

Practice Test

Word Reading

SAMPLE 1

A	wipe ○	wash ●	cloud ○
B	clothes ●	town ○	soup ○
C	close ○	heard ○	clean ●

SAMPLE 2

D	feed ●	blow ○	bird ○
E	basket ○	catch ○	bowl ●
F	dipper ○	kitchen ●	fancy ○

1	hurt ○	music ●	lizard ○
2	munch ○	dreams ○	drums ●
3	stir ○	listen ●	bean ○

4	shaping ○	grows ○	market ●
5	shouting ○	shopping ●	chart ○
6	food ●	marker ○	foot ○

GO ON

Name

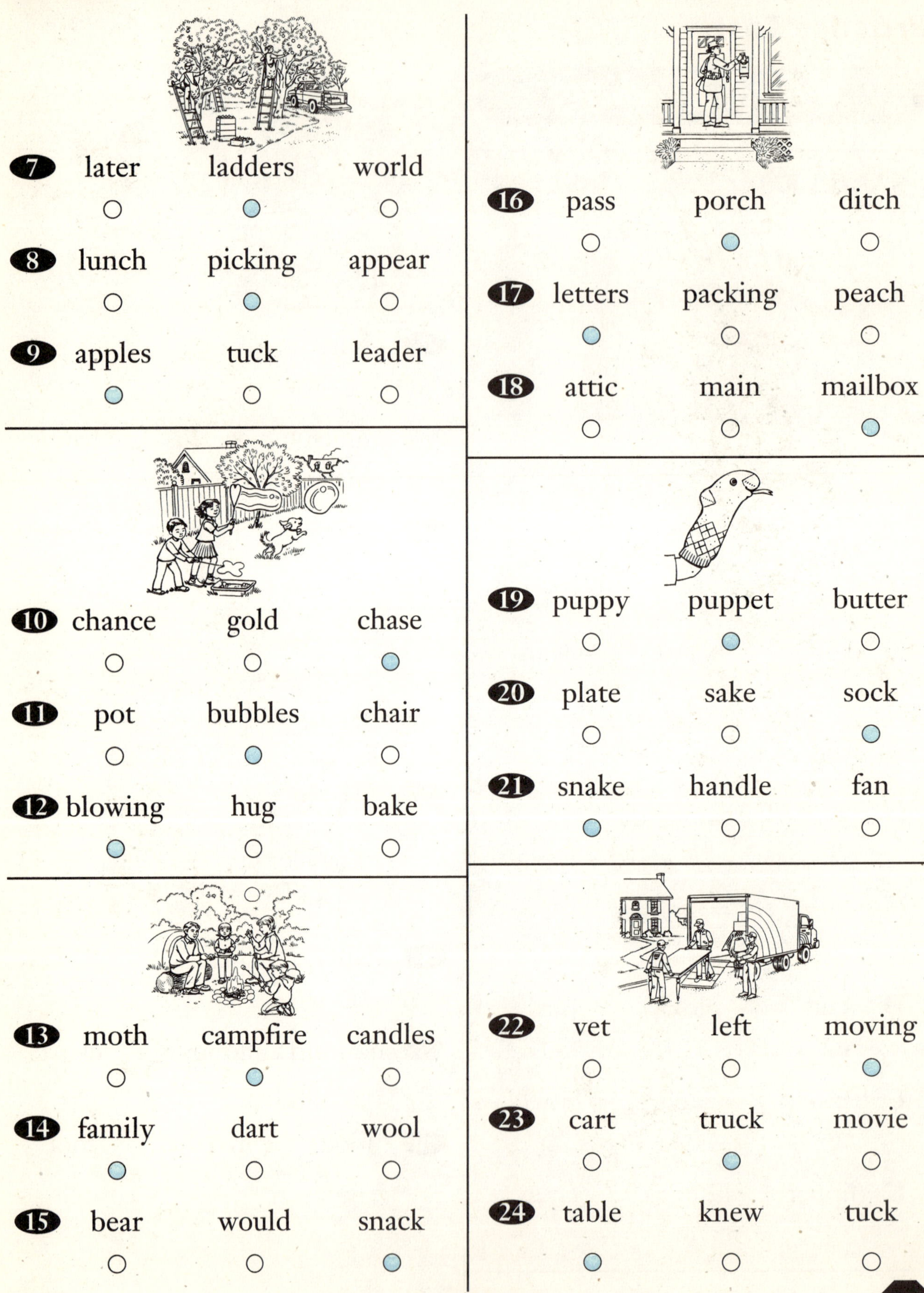

7 later ladders world

8 lunch picking appear

9 apples tuck leader

10 chance gold chase

11 pot bubbles chair

12 blowing hug bake

13 moth campfire candles

14 family dart wool

15 bear would snack

16 pass porch ditch

17 letters packing peach

18 attic main mailbox

19 puppy puppet butter

20 plate sake sock

21 snake handle fan

22 vet left moving

23 cart truck movie

24 table knew tuck

STOP

Name ______________________

Word Study Skills

SAMPLE A	SAMPLE B
○ pencil	○ cleans
● anyone	○ cleaned
○ longest	● cleaning

1.
- ○ ducklings
- ○ children
- ● inside

2.
- ● sometime
- ○ fluttering
- ○ meadows

3.
- ○ reading
- ● doghouse
- ○ skipping

4.
- ● everything
- ○ tightly
- ○ letters

5.
- ○ waiting
- ● waits
- ○ waited

6.
- ● clearly
- ○ clearer
- ○ clearest

7.
- ○ sails
- ○ sailing
- ● sailed

8.
- ○ slower
- ○ slowly
- ● slowest

STOP

Name

SAMPLE C

it's	hasn't	isn't
○	○	●

9

we've	we'd	we're
●	○	○

10

she's	she'll	she'd
●	○	○

11

wasn't	won't	weren't
○	○	●

12

I'll	I've	I'd
○	○	●

SAMPLE D

lamp

grow	lake	boxes
○	●	○

SAMPLE E

bird

hurt	bite	field
●	○	○

13 **wish**

shout	who	wave
○	○	●

14 **gray**

sleepy	late	began
○	●	○

15 **egg**

kept	joke	new
●	○	○

GO ON

Name ______________________________

16 **blink**

bins ○ | blue ● | lack ○

17 **moon**

boot ● | look ○ | door ○

18 **these**

chose ○ | mat ○ | father ●

19 **bread**

beach ○ | deep ○ | said ●

20 **wear**

hear ○ | chair ● | heat ○

21 **climb**

slide ● | clip ○ | skirt ○

22 **count**

low ○ | could ○ | shower ●

23 **gerbil**

goat ○ | page ● | frog ○

24 **chirp**

slip ○ | push ○ | each ●

25 **treat**

train ● | toast ○ | timer ○

STOP

Name

Reading Comprehension

SAMPLE A

It has hands.
It is a toy.

1 It helps you write.
You can carry it.

2 It helps keep you cool.
It goes on your head.

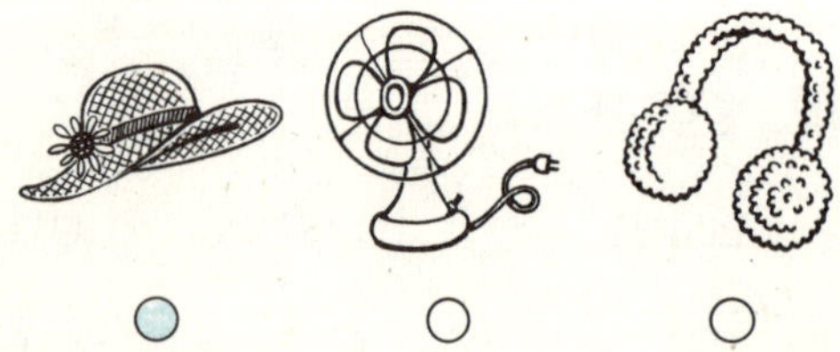

3 It is hot.
You can eat it.

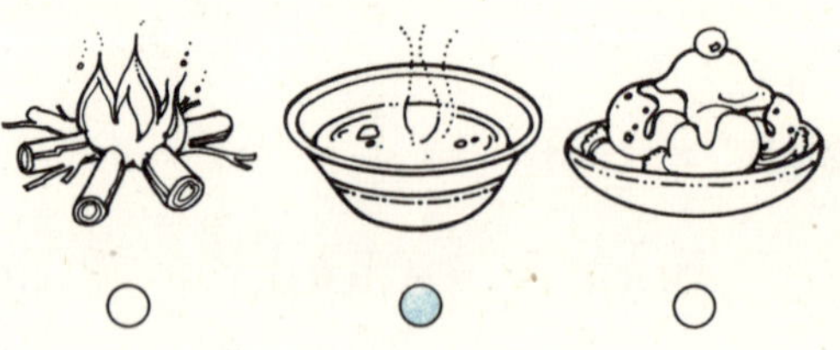

4 It has keys.
You can play it.

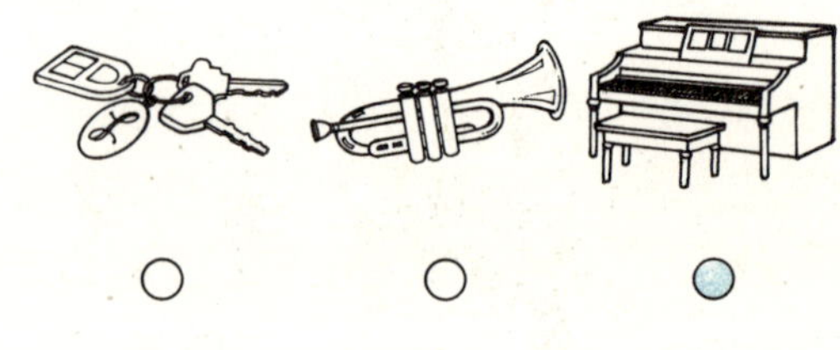

5 It has a shell.
It has four legs.

STOP

Name

SAMPLE

B Here is a

car truck table.

○ ● ○

C It can

walk jump move.

○ ○ ●

6 The children are playing

dress-up jump rope ball.

● ○ ○

7 Tom is wearing Dad's

watch coat socks.

○ ● ○

8 Nora's hat has a big

bow button feather.

○ ○ ●

9 Dad and Marta have a

tire road hammer.

● ○ ○

10 They are making a

bench house swing

○ ○ ●

11 in the

flower tree board.

○ ● ○

GO ON

Name

12 **Mother and Peter are at the**

mall mountain beach.

13 **They have been**

playing running shopping.

14 **Mother is carrying some**

baskets bags bins.

15 **Lyna is**

sleeping sweeping sitting.

16 **She is using a**

broom rake handle

17 **to clean the**

room hall steps.

Name

SAMPLE

The Horse Show

A horse show came to town. There were many big horses in the show. They jumped over fences. They raced each other. The crowd yelled and clapped.

D What came to town?

- ○ A circus
- ○ A parade
- ○ A horse show

E All of the people watching

- ○ sat quietly
- ○ cheered
- ○ smiled.

Fun with Clay

Lily likes to play with clay. She made small bowls to give to her mom and dad. She also made many circus animals out of clay. She gave them to her brother for his birthday. Everyone in Lily's family loves Lily's presents.

18 Lily knows how to make

puppets	gifts	cakes.
○	○	○

19 This story tells what Lily

- ○ likes to eat
- ○ likes to read
- ○ likes to make.

20 Lily likes to make things for her

family	friends	teacher.
○	○	○

GO ON

Name

Fred Packs a Bag

Fred was packing a big bag.

"I need to take these books," he said to himself. "I want to read a story to Grandmother. I think I will put in these drawings. They will show Grandfather what I have been doing in school. I also want to show him my new puzzle."

"Wow, that is a big bag!" said Dad. "You are only going to be there for one night."

"I know," said Fred. "But I have so much to share."

"Good thing we have lots of room in the backseat," said Dad. "We can put your suitcase there."

21 You can tell that Dad felt

- ○ sad
- ○ tired
- ○ surprised.

22 What did Fred want to share with his grandmother?

- ○ Some books
- ○ A puzzle
- ○ Some drawings

23 Fred is going to

- ○ a friend's home
- ○ his grandparents' home
- ○ his sister's home.

GO ON

Name ___

Making a Puppet

The children in Mrs. West's class wanted to make puppets. Mrs. West wrote down how to make them. This is the poster Mrs. West gave the class.

What You Need:

What You Do:

1. Draw and color a face on the bottom of the bag.
2. Cut paper strips for arms. Paste them onto the bag.
3. Cut yarn to make hair. Paste it in place.

24 The first thing to do is draw a face on the

- ○ back of the bag
- ○ side of the bag
- ● bottom of the bag.

25 Before pasting yarn on as hair, the children should

- ○ color the yarn
- ● cut the yarn
- ○ wind the yarn.

26 What did Mrs. West write?

- ● How to make a puppet
- ○ Why you should make a puppet
- ○ When you can make a puppet

GO ON

Name

Busy Beavers

Beavers are great builders. They use their sharp teeth to cut down trees. They use the trees to build dams across rivers and streams.

At the bottom of a dam, beavers place stones and mud. Then they put down logs. To keep things in place, they cover everything with mud, stones, and plants.

A deep pool forms behind the dam. There the beavers build their home, which is called a lodge.

27 The first step in making a dam is to

- ○ build a lodge
- ○ make a pool
- ○ cut down trees.

28 After the dam is finished, beavers build a

- ○ river
- ○ lodge
- ○ fort.

29 One thing beavers use to hold things in place is

- ○ mud
- ○ tape
- ○ water.

STOP

Name ____________________

Spelling

SAMPLE A

theer	there	ther
○	●	○

SAMPLE B

shout	shaut	showt
●	○	○

1	agen ○	agenn ○	again ●
2	blue ●	bloo ○	blou ○
3	allways ○	always ●	alwaz ○
4	eny ○	uny ○	any ●
5	trunk ●	trunck ○	trunc ○
6	sorrey ○	sory ○	sorry ●
7	hirt ○	hurt ●	hert ○
8	cair ○	care ●	kare ○
9	sircus ○	cirkus ○	circus ●
10	fish ●	fich ○	fis ○
11	gru ○	grew ●	groo ○
12	parth ○	pard ○	part ●
13	drink ●	drinc ○	drinck ○
14	paj ○	page ●	paje ○

GO ON

Name ____________________

15	caike ○	cake ●	kake ○
16	while ●	whille ○	hwile ○
17	reech ○	reche ○	reach ●
18	priz ○	prise ○	prize ●
19	chanj ○	change ●	chanje ○
20	cabin ●	kabin ○	caben ○
21	caul ○	call ●	coll ○
22	catch ●	catsh ○	cath ○
23	dishis ○	dishs ○	dishes ●
24	geting ○	getting ●	geteng ○
25	savved ○	saved ●	savd ○
26	toys ●	toyes ○	toies ○
27	giveing ○	givving ○	giving ●
28	running ●	runing ○	runneng ○
29	grapse ○	grapes ●	graps ○
30	sees ●	seez ○	seaz ○

STOP

Name ____________________

Language

SAMPLE A

My sister's name is <u>helen.</u>

- ○ helen?
- ● Helen.
- ○ The way it is

SAMPLE B

The boys <u>were</u> on time.

- ○ was
- ○ is
- ● The way it is

1 **Have you seen my <u>skates.</u>**

- ○ Skates!
- ● skates?
- ○ The way it is

2 **I am going to camp in <u>july.</u>**

- ● July.
- ○ july?
- ○ The way it is

3 **My teacher <u>said</u> we're going on a class trip.**

- ○ Said
- ○ say
- ● The way it is

4 **The boy <u>runs</u> in a race last week.**

- ● ran
- ○ runned
- ○ The way it is

GO ON

Name

5 **Where did you put my <u>hat.</u>**

- ○ Hat!
- ● hat?
- ○ The way it is

6 **Last week my aunt <u>came</u> for dinner.**

- ○ come
- ○ have come
- ● The way it is

7 **The children <u>taked</u> some apples for a snack.**

- ● took
- ○ takes
- ○ The way it is

8 **Joan usually <u>drew</u> a picture and then writes a story.**

- ● draws
- ○ draw
- ○ The way it is

9 **Watch out! That ladder is not <u>safe?</u>**

- ○ Safe?
- ● safe!
- ○ The way it is

10 **I have a piano lesson every <u>monday.</u>**

- ● Monday.
- ○ Monday?
- ○ The way it is

11 **My grandparents live in <u>New York.</u>**

- ○ New york?
- ○ new york.
- ● The way it is

12 **The boy <u>keeping</u> his toys in a big box.**

- ○ keeped
- ● kept
- ○ The way it is

STOP

Name

SAMPLE C

The turtle crawled. Across the road.

- ○ The turtle crawled across the road.
- ○ The turtle crawling across the road.
- ○ The way it is

SAMPLE D

The children play with the puppy.

- ○ The children playing with the puppy.
- ○ The children played. With the puppy.
- ○ The way it is

13 **Late last night. We saw an owl in the woods.**

- ○ Late last night we saw an owl. In the woods.
- ○ Late last night we saw an owl in the woods.
- ○ The way it is

14 **The hens scratching in the dirt looking for food.**

- ○ The hens are scratching in the dirt looking for food.
- ○ The hens scratching in the dirt. Looking for food.
- ○ The way it is

15 **Dad goes jogging. Before work each day.**

- ○ Each day. Before work Dad goes jogging.
- ○ Dad goes jogging before work each day.
- ○ The way it is

16 **Sandy wants to go bike riding on Saturday.**

- ○ Sandy wants to go bike riding. On Saturday.
- ○ Sandy wanting to go bike riding on Saturday.
- ○ The way it is

STOP

 Name

SAMPLE

Ants are found almost everywhere. They live in groups called colonies. Some ant colonies can be found underground. Colonies can also be found inside trees, under logs, or in mounds of earth.

E Which of these would go best after the last sentence?

- ○ Most ants are black, brown, or red.
- ○ An ant's body has three main parts.
- ● Colonies of ants can even make nests from tree leaves.

F Why was this story written?

- ○ To tell why ants bite and sting
- ● To tell where some ants live
- ○ To tell about an ant's body

Story 1

Many children have fun collecting interesting objects. Some collect small stuffed animals. Stamps, stickers, and trading cards are also popular things to collect. Some children collect things from nature such as shells, small pebbles, or feathers.

17 Which of these would go best after the last sentence?

- ○ That boy has a huge baseball card collection.
- ○ A box is a good place to keep big things such as model planes and cars.
- ● Collecting can be a fun way to spend free time.

18 Why was this story written?

- ● To tell about things that children collect
- ○ To tell where to find trading cards
- ○ To tell how to keep a collection neat

Name ____________________

Story 2

Beth got a pair of skates for a present. She also got a helmet and some pads. Before Beth could skate, her parents made her promise that she would always wear her helmet and pads. She also had to promise that she would not skate in the street.

19 Why was this story written?

- ○ To tell where to skate
- ● To tell how Beth will skate safely
- ○ To tell how to learn to skate

20 Which of these would not go with this story?

- ● Beth always wears a helmet when she rides a bike.
- ○ There are many safe places to skate in the park near Beth's house.
- ○ Beth's dad took her to skate in a park.

Story 3

Airplanes carry people and goods all over the world. Some airplanes are very small. They hold only one or two people. Other airplanes are large. They can carry hundreds of people and thousands of pounds of goods. Some of the biggest airplanes even have two floors.

21 Why was this story written?

- ○ To tell the cost of an airplane ride
- ○ To tell how fast an airplane can go
- ● To tell about different kinds of airplanes

22 Which of these would go best after the last sentence?

- ● These large planes are called air buses.
- ○ Have you ever ridden on an airplane?
- ○ Airplanes have been around for a long time.

STOP

Name ______________________________

SAMPLE G

- ● bed
- ○ lamp
- ○ radio

23
- ○ yarn
- ● fruit
- ○ window

24
- ○ rock
- ○ ribbon
- ● rain

25
- ● grass
- ○ today
- ○ red

26
- ● paddle
- ○ plant
- ○ pond

27
- ○ net
- ○ tree
- ● goat

28
- ○ sweet
- ● six
- ○ snack

STOP

Name

Listening

SAMPLE A

- ○ push
- ○ talk to
- ○ touch

1
- ○ ride
- ○ fix
- ○ see

2
- ○ hold
- ○ throw
- ○ put

3
- ○ drawing
- ○ meal
- ○ mistake

4
- ○ do
- ○ find
- ○ give

5
- ○ walk
- ○ run
- ○ bath

6
- ○ hungry
- ○ wild
- ○ sleeping

7
- ○ sad
- ○ happy
- ○ well

8
- ○ half
- ○ whole
- ○ hot

9
- ○ rest
- ○ cook
- ○ play

10
- ○ talk to
- ○ excuse
- ○ sing to

GO ON

Name

SAMPLE B

SAMPLE C

11

12

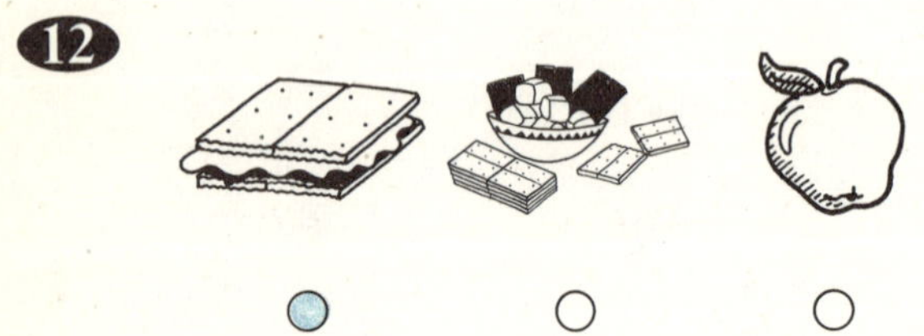

13

14

15

16

GO ON

Name

SAMPLE D

- ○ Katy's dog
- ● Katy's friend
- ○ Katy's sister

SAMPLE E

- ○ "Katy's Pet Cat"
- ● "Katy's Lost Homework"
- ○ "Katy and Nelia"

17
- ○ To give directions
- ● To tell a story
- ○ To tell how to do a job

18
- ○ trust her dog
- ○ eat snacks
- ● take better care of her homework

19
- ○ Artists who fold paper
- ● The art of folding paper
- ○ A Japanese food

20
- ● It is very old.
- ○ You use metal to do it.
- ○ No one can do it today.

21
- ○ No one did origami.
- ● More people started to do origami.
- ○ A man made origami animals.

22
- ○ Sad
- ○ Mad
- ● Happy

23
- ● To come to the party
- ○ To practice the piano
- ○ To do her homework

GO ON

Name

24 ○ A story
○ A recipe
○ Directions

25 ○ Jason
○ Sam
○ Aunt Gail

26 ○ Maria
○ Dawn
○ Maria's mother

27 ○ "Baby Pictures"
○ "Maria's Eyes"
○ "Maria's Sister"

28 ○ Alaska
○ Nevada
○ California

29 ○ Tell everyone about the gold
○ Find the gold
○ Govern the state of California

30 ○ They followed their families.
○ They wanted to see the gold.
○ They wanted to get rich.

STOP